DIY
WEDDING
MANUAL

Haynes

THE STEP-BY-STEP GUIDE TO CREATING YOUR PERFECT WEDDING DAY ON A BUDGET

LAURA STRUTT

Contents

Introduction

Congratulations! You're getting married!

So, now that the giddiness of the proposal has passed, or at least once your legs no longer feel like they're made of jelly, you'll be turning your thoughts to wedding planning. For some people, the prospect of wedding planning is exciting, perhaps having dreamt of this special day since childhood. For others, however, this can be a really daunting experience. I mean, there is so much to do, so many things to organise, so many people to think of and... did I mention, there is so much to do?

With the reported costs of the average wedding soaring, it's no wonder that many brides and grooms-to-be are turning away from the big budget blowout wedding and opting for a more personal, less costly celebration. Every couple wants their day to be unique and special, and for many hand-making all or some of the elements for the Big Day is the perfect opportunity to stamp their individual personalities on the event.

As a couple, my husband and I are pretty hands-on, creative folks, so for us creating many of the different elements for our wedding was a natural choice. The journey from our engagement to our wedding day (under 12 months) was magical, and whilst we were making things that would later form part of our special day, we were also making memories during the planning and preparations. We managed to create a wedding that came in under a quarter of the quoted national average cost, and had great fun doing it! I want to show other brides that with a little inspiration, and armed with a few crafty supplies, they too can get a dreamy wedding that suits their budget.

Whether you want to keep the costs down by doing it yourself, or you fancy adding a creative flourish to the proceedings; whether you handcraft a few key elements or create the entire kit and caboodle with your own fair hands, this guide will help you along the way. The wedding projects here are designed to show you a few crafty techniques and ideas for making some of the essential elements for your special day; from invitations and table menus, veils and bouquets to centrepieces and cake decorations.

We all have a different sense of style, love different colours and want to create different things, so the projects in this book can all be created as they are, worked up in different shades and tones or even used simply as inspiration or to help glean some crafty skills. Guidance is also given regarding how long to allow for each project, and the likely cost (at the time of writing).

Aside from hand-making items there are lots of other tasks that you'll need to attend to on the journey from newly engaged to newlywed. You'll need to make plans for the ceremony and the reception, and there are guests to think of, food to serve and a bridal party to pick – to name but a few of the tasks that lie ahead. With so many things to consider and arrange it's no wonder that many couples start to feel like ripping their hair out! To help save you from feeling as though your To Do List is getting the better of you, this guide also looks over the different elements that make up a wedding, to help you through the process of selecting readings for your service, picking transportation, choosing a wedding photographer and setting a theme for the Big Day – and everything in between! Along the way you'll find a wealth of practical tips and hints on organisation, setting budgets and staying on top of the preparations.

Happy planning!

Laura Strutt

Laura Strutt
Spring 2014

First published February 2014

A catalogue record for this book is available
from the British Library

ISBN 978 0 85733 381 0

Library of Congress control no. 2013955821

Haynes Publishing,
Sparkford, Yeovil, Somerset BA22 7JJ, UK
Tel: +44 (0) 1963 442030
Fax: +44 (0) 1963 440001
E-mail: sales@haynes.co.uk
Website: www.haynes.co.uk

Haynes North America, Inc.,
861 Lawrence Drive, Newbury Park,
California 91320, USA

Printed in the USA by Odcombe Press LP,
1299 Bridgestone Parkway, La Vergne, TN 37086

Author:	Laura Strutt
Project Manager:	Louise McIntyre
Copy editor:	Ian Heath
Design and layout:	James Robertson
Wedding Photography:	Kerrie Mitchell
	www.kerriemitchell.co.uk
Project Photography:	Thomas F J Ford
	www.thomasfjford.com
Stock photos:	Shutterstock

Author acknowledgements

There are a number of people that have made the writing of
this book possible:
   Kerrie Mitchell for her exceptional photography skills that
transformed our wedding day and have added delight to the
pages of this book.
   To my dear family and in-laws; the Styles, Cruickshank
and Coomber families, and the Strutt, Foulkes, Newton,
Blackmore and Kennedy families, who've all listened, given
advice and guidance on weddings (our own and in this book)
for the best part of two years!
   And, last but by no means least, my husband John Strutt,
for without him having made me the best offer of my life and
then becoming my husband on the 15 September 2012,
I would never have experienced the magic of creating our own
wonderful DIY wedding day.

Chapter 1

Planning and preparation

Whether you know exactly what you want for your Big Day, or you don't know where to begin, the secret to getting off to a flying start is to commence by dedicating a little time to the planning and preparations. Here you'll discover how to set your budget and create your own wedding countdown, plus essential tips and hints for a stress-free DIY wedding celebration.

Getting started

Find out where to begin your wedding planning with this quick-start guide.

www.kerriemitchell.co.uk

Every wedding is different, and that's the beauty of them. As a couple you'll be deciding on a number of elements over the coming months to create a day to remember. Whatever your budget or your style, there are a few things that all soon-to-be brides and grooms need to think about.

As with any task, breaking wedding planning down into a series of separate elements will make arranging the event – big or small – manageable. You may have already talked in depth about the type of wedding you'd like – the theme, the location – and you may even have the finer points decided, from style of cake to colours for the bridesmaids' dresses.

www.kerriemitchell.co.uk

However, many couples take some time out in the early stages to talk about the overall logistics, their expectations and, most importantly, the budget.

Identify your wedding style

Grab a notebook and pen and run through these questions to get to grips with creating your wedding style:

- Do you want a religious or a civil ceremony?
- What season do you want to get married in – do you dream of being a summer bride or hosting a winter wedding?
- Do you want a very traditional day, or are you inspired by an informal event?
- Do you want to declare your partnership in front of your extended family and wide circle of friends, or are you keen on a more intimate celebration?
- Do you have a preferred date – or even day in mind – or are you flexible about the date of your marriage?

Some of these answers will come more quickly than others, and some will get answered along the way. You may also find – particularly if you're working to a budget – that decisions you make in planning your day will answer many of these questions for you.

HAPPINESS IS NOT A DESTINATION. IT IS A WAY OF LIFE.

www.kerriemitchell.co.uk

What is a bridal party?

Traditionally there are a number of different roles in a wedding, collectively known as the 'bridal party'. Here's a rundown of the main roles and an outline of their respective duties and responsibilities.

Bride and Groom – Aside from being responsible for exchanging vows, the bride will select the bridesmaids and the groom will choose the best man and any ushers.

Father of the Bride – Traditionally this man would be paying for the celebrations. However, modern weddings are now funded in a range of ways. Many brides are walked down the aisle by their fathers, and he may also make toasts and give speeches during the wedding breakfast.

Mother of the Bride – Chiefly responsible for assisting with planning and preparations for the day, her role has developed over the years, with many Mums providing a reading or giving a speech at the reception.

Father of the Groom – In more recent years the groom's father has been taking a more active role on the day, often assisting the father of the bride in the hosting and toasting elements of the reception.

Mother of the Groom – Modern couples rely on the groom's mother as much as the bride's mother for assistance with planning the wedding.

Best Man – The groom's right-hand man. He'll assist with a number of different tasks before the event, including arranging or assisting with the stag party preparations. He'll help out in the running of the day and, traditionally, gives a speech at the wedding breakfast.

Ushers – These are male (and sometimes female) family members or close friends, nominated by the groom and best man. They'll assist the best man in the running of the day, ensuring the comfort of the guests.

Chief Bridesmaid (sometimes called 'maid of honour') – Selected by the bride, this is usually a sister or best friend, who'll give assistance with planning. She'll often help to select the wedding dress and plan the hen night. On the day, she'll liaise with the best man to ensure the event runs smoothly.

Bridesmaids – A collection of female siblings, relatives or friends that provide support and assistance to the bride in the months before the wedding, and help the chief bridesmaid on the day.

Pageboy – A small child, often a family member, who walks behind the bride assisting with the lengths of her flowing dress, depending on the style of the wedding – and the bride's dress! A pageboy and flower girl may often walk down the aisle ahead of the bride.

Flower Girl – A small child, often a relative, who walks down the aisle before the bride, carrying flowers. This is a fantastic role for a child too young to be a bridesmaid as, after walking down the aisle, they're able to return to sit with their family for the ceremony.

Ring Bearer – Commonly a small child, who carries the two wedding rings secured on a pillow or in a bag or a box. Modern weddings often have the best man take responsibility for the rings – or you could even have your favourite pet dog perform the duties (with the officiant's consent).

Witnesses – You'll be required to have two witnesses to sign the wedding register along with yourselves. This contributes to the legal aspect of the ceremony.

Modern weddings, even the more formal affairs, can take a more relaxed approach to the bridal party meaning that, for the most part, you're able to select the roles you want to incorporate into your own wedding.

Setting a budget

Understand how to set a wedding budget that suits you and your lifestyle.

When it comes to money, we all have different ideas of what's expensive and what we can afford to spend. The budget you have for your celebrations will be something that is unique to you. If you've always dreamed of a fairytale wedding, your budget being on the small side doesn't mean your dreams will be dashed. Using a little creativity and some DIY know-how you'll discover that even if you have Champagne tastes but a lemonade budget, you can still have a wonderful wedding.

Laura's Bride Guide

Is there a secret to keeping your wedding within your budget? Well, sadly I can't wave a magic wand and get your dream wedding for a fraction of the cost, but I can share a few tips on how to save money by doing some things yourself. If you want to have a three-course sit-down meal and an orchestra playing at your reception I won't be the one to tell you that you shouldn't have it. But, if you're paying for it – and trying to keep within a budget – decide if it's something you *really* want. Some elements might be fashionable, or things that you've seen at other weddings, but my personal rule is, if you don't love it, ask yourself 'Do I really need it?' It might sound harsh, but it'll help you to stay on top of costs.

Before you make any payments, consider a few things. If you're buying in bulk, cost out the amount you need – a £1 item might sound cheap until you remember that you want 800 of them! Take time to think – impulsive decisions can often be expensive ones; if you have time, shop around, see if you can find something similar at a better price for you. Remember, using your creative resources can help to keep costs down – so ask around, you never know who might be able to offer services or help.

Why set a budget?

So, why do you need to set a budget? If you have a nice little nest egg tucked away in a savings account, why do you need to decide on a budget for the overall event? Surely, having a set amount of money means that you won't over- or under-spend, right? Wrong! As there are so many components to each wedding, it can be all too easy to spend out on one element and completely overlook another. It might not be the best start to married life if you've stepped out in a couture gown that cost a hefty chunk of your budget whilst your husband has had to dust off his old (and likely dated) interview suit!

Though there's no right or wrong way to spend your wedding budget, there will doubtless be some things that you simply won't want included in your wedding, whilst there are others that you can't live without. It's impossible for you to know exactly how much everything will cost in the early stages, so the best way to begin is by working through the budget checklist opposite. Start by deleting the items that aren't appropriate to you. Working through this list you can decide which elements are more important to you than others – the things that you're prepared to, or expect to, spend more money on. This'll help to give you an outline of how to keep on top of your spending.

Your wedding budget checklist

Keep on top of your spending and avoid any nasty surprises with this handy budget guide.

Begin by working through this list. Cross out the items that simply don't apply to you. Add the total of your wedding fund to the top of your list. Work through and decide which items are a priority for you; some you may not even want to include, while there maybe other things that aren't listed but you've always dreamed of... that hot air balloon ride into the sunset as husband and wife, for example. Add them to the list to take it into consideration when dividing up your budget! Knowing how much you've allocated to each element will help control your spending; then once you start making payments, work back over the list, adding in the actual amounts spent – if you've gone over budget on one section you'll be able to identify areas to cut back on, or if you're under budget you can decide if there are areas to which you can transfer the remaining funds.

Laura's Bride Guide

Dividing your budget between the different aspects of your wedding is, strictly speaking, not something you can get wrong or right. Of course, if you only set aside £50 to feed a 600-strong guest list you'll certainly have your work cut out! But combine a little common sense and creativity and you'll be able to get your budget to cover all the bases. To ensure that we spent our money wisely, we worked through the list and decided what was important for us. Agreeing on the important aspects for your own wedding will help you to realise the things that you aren't worried about including.

.... & ....

Date .... Total budget £ ....

Item	Amount allocated	Actual spent
Ceremony	£..............	£..............
Reception	£..............	£..............
Wedding gown	£..............	£..............
Bridal accessories	£..............	£..............
Groom's suit	£..............	£..............
Groom's accessories	£..............	£..............
Best man's attire	£..............	£..............
Groomsmen's attire	£..............	£..............
Chief bridesmaid's dress	£..............	£..............
Bridesmaids' attire	£..............	£..............
Pageboy's attire	£..............	£..............
Flower girl's attire	£..............	£..............
Decoration for venues	£..............	£..............
Transport	£..............	£..............
Reception drinks	£..............	£..............
Catering for the reception	£..............	£..............
Music for the reception	£..............	£..............
Photography & videography	£..............	£..............
Flowers	£..............	£..............
Corsages	£..............	£..............
Gifts for the wedding party	£..............	£..............
Honeymoon	£..............	£..............
Other	£..............	£..............
Other	£..............	£..............

Contracts and negotiating

With weddings comes paperwork. Discover how to keep on top of it.

The majority of weddings – particularly those that have DIY elements – will work with a number of different suppliers, from caterers, and florists to musicians and photographers. When securing a booking for each element you'll often be presented with a contract. These documents can be daunting, but be sure to read and understand them before signing on the dotted line.

Getting to grips with contracts

There's no way round it – you'll need to read through all contracts carefully. A contract is, essentially, a written agreement that links goods or services in exchange for money. They're designed to protect both parties. Taking the time to carefully run through the sections will ensure not only that you understand them, but also that you're happy with them and know just what to expect on the day. You can also make a note of any further questions that you might have for the supplier.

Parting with payments

As with most products or services, you'll often be required to pay a deposit in order to secure the item for your required date – this is standard practice for weddings too. I would always recommend that you review the contract or terms before parting with any money – you don't want to lose a non-refundable deposit simply because you haven't reviewed the details fully. Reputable suppliers often agree to a 'goodwill' period in which

they secure the date or reserve the products, allowing you time to fully review the details of the contract before finalising with the payment of a deposit.

Once the deposit has been paid the services will be secured and then the final balance will need to be met later. Some suppliers require the balance in one payment prior to the wedding date, while others request it over a couple of instalments. Many suppliers send reminders – a letter, an email or even, in some cases, a phone call – to remind you about the upcoming payments. However, adding the due dates of payments to your calendar will help you to keep on top of things as life gets busier and the Big Day approaches.

Time to haggle

For some people haggling is something that comes naturally, and if this is one of your strengths it will certainly help keep things within budget! However, always remember that if you're intending to haggle on the price do so before you sign a contract or pay the deposit – this ensures that both parties are happy with the final agreement and that there's no feeling of ill-will. It's important to remember that some suppliers simply won't be able to give you a discount. In these cases look over the proposed package or selection of services to see if all of the elements listed are essential – for instance, do you really have your heart set on a course of sorbet at the wedding breakfast? Many suppliers are happy to remove items or elements of a package and adjust the price accordingly to suit your requirements, so be sure to discuss the options in advance.

Laura's Bride Guide

A notebook is essential for a bride – jotting down everything from ideas, guest lists, favourite websites, quotes and contact numbers will prove worth its weight in gold. As you start to research venues, photographers and menu suggestions your notebook will soon become a bit of a jumble. A folder or expandable file is a great piece of kit when it comes to wedding planning. Section-off different areas for each element of your wedding – this'll make it easier to compare costs, keep on top of payments and save you from tearing your hair out!

Your wedding countdown

Using the time in the run-up to your wedding wisely, to stay on top of all the tasks.

There's a saying that you should be engaged for six months before you get hitched. Whilst this might be wise romantic advice, it's also pretty practical, giving you at least 26 weeks to organise a wedding. If you have a full 24 months you'll have to double the length of this timeline to suit your schedule. Nevertheless, time will pass much quicker than you think – getting in early with things like invitations and booking the venue, photographer or band is a smart way to avoid disappointment.

Some couples choose a short engagement, sometimes six months or even less. Getting a wedding arranged in a very short space of time isn't impossible, but it'll mean you have to take a different approach – for example, some options, like having a dress handmade for you, might not fit into a shorter timescale. Whether you opt for a long or short engagement, tailor this timeline to create your own personal wedding countdown.

12 months
- ❏ Decide on your budget.
- ❏ Consider dates – aim to get a shortlist of three to four possible dates.
- ❏ Research wedding venues and visit a selected shortlist.

11 months
- ❏ Select and inform your bridal party.
- ❏ Research photographers and videographers.
- ❏ Research catering options.

10 months
- ❏ Book ceremony and reception venues.
- ❏ Start researching wedding attire for bride, groom and bridal party.
- ❏ Send out 'Save The Date' cards.

9 months

❑ Select your wedding rings.

❑ Consider wedding themes and colours.

❑ Book wedding photographer and videographer.

8 months

❑ Finalise wedding dress.

❑ Research florist and caterers.

❑ Organise the details of the ceremony with the officiant; select readings and music.

❑ Research wedding bands and DJs.

❑ Research bridesmaids' attire.

7 months

❑ Book wedding transport.

❑ Book caterers and florists.

❑ Research groom and groomsmen's attire.

❑ Arrange accommodation, if required, for the wedding night; where possible arrange block bookings for guests.

❑ Create wedding gift registry.

6 months

❑ Wedding dress fitting – select additional bridal accessories, underwear, shoes and veil.

❑ Send out wedding invitations.

❑ Finalise groom and groomsmen's attire.

❑ Finalise bridesmaids' attire.

5 months

❑ Research hair and make-up artists for bride and book trial.

❑ Assist mother of the bride and mother of the groom to select wedding outfits.

❑ Research wedding cakes.

4 months

❑ Plan and book stag and hen parties.

❑ Book wedding bands and DJs.

❑ Research honeymoons.

3 months

❑ Order wedding cake.

❑ Book honeymoon.

8 weeks

❑ Confirm guest numbers with venues and caterers.

❑ Begin creating seating plans.

7 weeks

❑ Attend stag and hen nights.

❑ Groom and best man to prepare speeches.

6 weeks
❑ Plan rehearsal dinner or pre-wedding event.

5 weeks
❑ Select presents for the bridal party.
❑ Review and confirm all bookings and schedule any final payments.

4 weeks
❑ Final fittings for wedding dresses, groom's suit and bridal party attire.
❑ Attend bridal hair and make-up trial.
❑ Schedule pre-wedding hair and beauty treatments.

3 weeks
❑ Finalise seating plan and inform caterer.
❑ Groom and best man to finalise speeches.

2 weeks
❑ Groom haircut and any pre-wedding beauty treatments.
❑ Collect wedding dress, groom's suit and wedding party attire.

1 week
❑ Bride's pre-wedding hair and beauty treatments.
❑ Confirm arrangements for flowers and cakes.

6 days
❑ If you're heading off on honeymoon directly after the wedding, confirm all booking, arrange transportation and currency and pack.

5 days
❑ Select bride and groom's going-away outfits.

4 days
❑ Attend pre-wedding beauty appointments.

3 days
❑ Water your houseplants – chances are they're feeling pretty neglected by now!

2 days
❑ Lie out or pack all wedding attire, cosmetics and going-away outfits.

1 day
❑ Plan a day of non-wedding time spent relaxing with your fiancé, family and friends.

Your wedding day!
❑ Enjoy your special day!

Wedding traditions

There are a few wedding-day customs that make fabulous accents and create brilliant memories.

We've all heard the phrase 'something old, something new, something borrowed and something blue'. These items are traditionally given to or worn by the bride on her wedding day as a token of good luck. This tradition is the perfect opportunity to get really sentimental, if you're that way inclined, or to add a dash of your own sparkling personality. Every bride that embraces this tradition will do something a little different to the next – there's no right or wrong – so, why not pick out something fun, meaningful or special?

Something old
Vintage jewellery is a fantastic element to add to your wedding, whatever style of dress or wedding theme you've selected. Heirloom jewellery is often too special for everyday wear, so this is the perfect opportunity to bring it out and make the most of it.

www.kerriemitchell.co.uk

▲ I wore a pearl ring left to me by my Granny and a pearl necklace from my Mum on my wedding day. Picking out sentimental items is not only special to those close to you, but vintage pieces will gain lots of compliments on the day.

▼ You don't want to be carrying about a huge handbag on your wedding day, so a vintage evening bag is ideal. Not only will it be unique and stunning, it'll be just the right size for a few essentials, without looking cumbersome. Check out your local charity shops, vintage fairs and even search online to snap up a pretty bargain.

www.kerriemitchell.co.uk

www.kerriemitchell.co.uk

Something new

▲ Shoes are often an indulgence for a bride, and this is the perfect opportunity to step out in something really special. It's also a great way for brides on a budget to compromise on a designer gown and select really glamorous shoes!

Something borrowed

Many brides are 'lent' a lacy handkerchief for their wedding day. Not only is this a touching gesture, it's wonderfully practical too –

if you get caught up in the emotion you don't want to be searching about for a paper tissue.

▶ I borrowed a brooch from my Mother-in-law (to be) to accent my handmade bouquet. This is the time to ask your sister if you can borrow a bracelet you've always admired, or your friend if she can lend you her antique cameo necklace – after all, if you can't ask for these for your wedding day, when can you?

www.kerriemitchell.co.uk

Something blue

Adding an accent of blue can be done in so many different ways – some brides decide to pick blue shoes that just peep out from under the layers of their frothy wedding gowns, others select a garter with blue ribbons and trimmings.

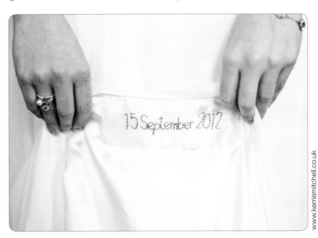

www.kerriemitchell.co.uk

▲ Carefully embroidering your wedding date on to satin ribbon to stitch to the hem or lining of your dress is not only a unique twist on the Something Blue tradition, but also transforms your wedding gown into an instant heirloom!

www.kerriemitchell.co.uk

▲ For an extra flash of colour I added a vintage blue swallow brooch to the comb when I made my birdcage wedding veil.

Laura's Bride Guide

As well as a tradition, the need to have items that are old, new, borrowed or blue is a really brilliant way to get family members and close friends involved in the planning and preparation for your wedding. Whatever wedding photography arrangements you make, be sure to ask the photographer to get some shots of these items at some stage in the day, to capture the memories.

Setting a theme

Use a theme to tie together the tone, style and overall mood of your wedding day.

For some couples, a theme is something that pops up instantly. Perhaps you have a common interest – a love for sci-fi movies, a passion for historical novels, or you both support the same sports team. These can be the basis for selecting your theme. You can then apply this to a greater or lesser extent to your decorations and the styling of your day.

Themes can also be set around colours. Selecting your favourite hues works as a great starting point for choosing stationery, dresses and accents. You can select a single shade, team two colours together or even work with a whole host of different colourways. The colour palettes you pick will help to bring together all the different elements of your wedding.

Feeling stumped for ideas?

Creating a little mood board with magazine cuttings, favourite quotes and sketches of ideas is a great way to identify the elements you'd like to include. A theme can be drawn from any aspect and applied to other elements to give a refined style. There might be something that you've already set your heart on for your wedding day – a powder blue camper van to arrive in, pink-iced cupcakes, a bouquet of bright orange gerberas. If you have a very definite idea of one element, then try using this as the basis to build your theme – you'll be surprised how quickly the ideas come together!

Colour palettes

Bold blush

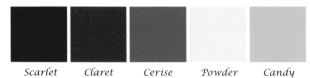

| Scarlet | Claret | Cerise | Powder | Candy |

Mixing up shades of reds with pinks is a fabulous way to inject some passion into your theme.

Elegant formals

| Storm | Battleship | Nude | Stone | Graphite |

Darker shades needn't be sombre. A collection of greys teamed with lighter accents – even glimmering silver – can create the glamour and sophistication of the Roaring Twenties.

Contemporary brights

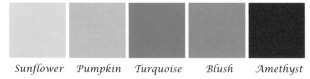

| Sunflower | Pumpkin | Turquoise | Blush | Amethyst |

These vibrant tones are both pretty and modern. Adding a cool splash of turquoise helps to keep the palette fresh.

Jewel tones

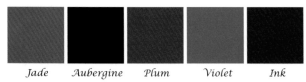

| Jade | Aubergine | Plum | Violet | Ink |

Rich and elegant, these colours ooze style and sophistication for the glamorous couple.

Vintage neutrals

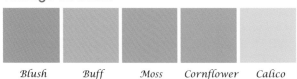

| Blush | Buff | Moss | Cornflower | Calico |

The muted tones of these colours are beautiful and timeless, and will team perfectly with heirloom-style dresses and vintage tea parties.

Fresh country

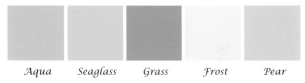

| Aqua | Seaglass | Grass | Frost | Pear |

A palette of cool and light colours is ideal for a spring or summer wedding. These tones are perfect for those who don't want a theme that's too girly.

Pretty feminine

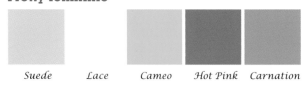

| Suede | Lace | Cameo | Hot Pink | Carnation |

Pink is a popular choice at weddings. Keep it contemporary with a blend of bright and pastel tones.

Laura's Bride Guide

Everyone's wedding is different. What worked for your best friend won't necessarily work for you. You might like the theme to be really rigid, with everything matching down to the last confetti petal and buttonhole; or you might take a more relaxed approach and just have a flash of your chosen colours on different elements.

Getting creative

Before you begin slicing paper, cutting fabric and threading beads with wild abandon, take time to consider a few things.

With any creative and hands-on task it's tempting to roll up your sleeves and get stuck in right away. Whilst I'd never want to be the one to stand in the way of inspiration, in the long run taking time to consider these key elements before you begin can save time, money and stress.

There will be a number of factors that'll help you to determine what elements are worth making yourself – including the timeframe, cost of supplies and the skills and experience that you already possess. It's also worth considering how many guests will be attending, the style of the venue and the theme of your Big Day. These will be different for every couple, and it's important to remember that ideas you have in these early stages can always be changed and updated as you continue the planning. That's the beauty of a DIY wedding – you can do whatever suits you!

Helping hands

If you've decided you don't have the time or experience to dedicate to one aspect of your wedding preparations, remember there are often folks that would be happy to lend a hand. Whether you're able to completely outsource an entire project, or recruit a team of chums to form a production line for the more laborious tasks, every little will help. Ask around – you'll be surprised how keen people will be to get involved and help out!

Time is of the essence

It's important to prioritise the projects you work on. For instance, it would be silly to create all the table plans and place markers before you've made and sent out the invitations – there may be people that can't attend, meaning you'd have to redo elements, which would be time-consuming and frustrating. So start out with a list of the items you want to make, and try to put them in the order in which they need to be completed. This will help you ascertain how long you have to dedicate to creating the components of your DIY wedding.

Your supplies

If you're already a keen crafter you'll probably have the benefit of an ample stash of papers, motifs, threads, stamps and inks, sugar-crafting tools, and beads and buttons. Not only will this be a great source of inspiration for everything from colour schemes to themes, using items that you already have will also help to shave pennies, and even pounds, from your budget. If you need to buy supplies be sure to check the amounts you require for each element before starting – there's nothing more frustrating than getting partway through a project only to realise that you need more glue, or that you don't have enough food colouring.

It can be worthwhile checking out local wholesalers, as buying in bulk can often be a budget-friendly solution. Hunt through markets and charity shops – these are great for picking up unusual items to add a unique touch to your decor, at a fraction of the cost of buying new!

No doubt you'll begin to amass a wide range of craft materials, tools and supplies, and if you're able to dedicate some space in your home to accommodate a makeshift studio that's perfect.

Stow items into neat storage boxes – this will help to keep everything in good condition and will ensure that it's ready to hand when you need it and makes transporting finished items to the venue much easier.

Laura's Bride Guide

One of the most challenging aspects of wedding planning is fitting everything into your no doubt already busy schedule, even more so if you're hand-making many of the elements. So, how do you even begin to know what you can achieve in the run-up to your wedding? Well, to try and make this task a little simpler I've set out an approximate timescale for each of the projects in this book. This'll help you to calculate how much time you'll need to dedicate to each element.

As your budget will often be at the forefront of your mind, there's also a rough guide on the prices per item. Using this information you'll be able to assess whether making 400 hand-embroidered silk napkins for your table settings – at £2.50 a pop, and each taking two hours to complete – is how you want to spend your time and money!

The skill factor

One key factor in hand crafting is your prior craft experience. The projects in this book have been designed with thorough step-by-step instructions, so that anyone can make them – regardless of experience. However, it's always worth bearing in mind your existing skills and using these to their greatest advantage whenever you can. If you've made your own Christmas cards without fail for the last ten years, then the prospect of making hundreds of invitations probably won't leave you feeling overwhelmed. On the flip side, if you've never sat behind a sewing machine you might want to give careful consideration to the idea of sewing your own bespoke wedding gown. Now, that's not to say that if you've never hand crafted before you should steer clear of making anything – quite the contrary. If you have your heart set on sewing your own dress, but lack the practical skills, ask around your family, soon-to-be in-laws and circle of friends; perhaps there's an avid seamstress that'll be on hand to assist. Many local craft stores offer workshops or drop-in sessions for everything from cardmaking and cake decorating to jewellery and sewing classes. Find out if there are any in your area that might help you to boost your skills and get your project under way without a hitch.

Your crafting kit

Depending on the projects that you undertake you'll require a selection of tools and equipment. Here's a collection of some of the items used within this book:

Coloured markers

Alphabet rubber stamps

Paper glue

Hot glue

Dressmaker's scissors

Paper scissors

Rubber stamp inks

Embroidery hoop

Tape

Selection of pens and pencils

Jewellery-making tools

Ruler

Hole punch

Creating a wedding day survival kit

Be prepared for (almost!) anything with a handy kit of disaster-averting essentials.

Chances are your wedding will go without a hitch. After all, by the time the day arrives you'll have spent a lot of time and energy planning and preparing, so all there is left to do is make your vows and have fun! That said, it's a great idea to collect together a few essentials, those 'just in case' items that might come in handy!

A travel sewing kit – especially one that has a selection of safety pins – is a must-have in your kit. It's great for any last-minute repairs or emergencies with the bridal party's garments. You may also want to pack the following:

- ❑ Spare tights/stockings
- ❑ Plasters
- ❑ Deodorant
- ❑ Essential make-up
- ❑ Lip balm
- ❑ Breath mints
- ❑ Mini hairspray
- ❑ Painkillers

Safety first

Some of the craft tools you'll use for making projects could have sharp points, moving parts, or might even operate at high temperatures. As with any project you work on, it's essential you use the tools with care to prevent injury. Most craft tools come with a user manual indicating the correct methods for using them safely. Always work on a clean, steady surface in good lighting and make use of protective equipment, like heat-resistant gloves and safety glasses.

Essential timings

Make a list of the running order, with times, for the day; on the reverse write out the names and contact information for all the suppliers. This can be printed out on to pieces of card and given to the best man and the chief bridesmaid should they be needed to help out on the day.

Chapter 2

Spreading
the word

Telling your family and friends about your exciting upcoming nuptials involves
a lot more than simply sharing your great news. It's also essential in making sure
your guests are formally invited, providing information about the occasion and
helping to finalise the guest list. Here you'll discover how to make, create and get
on top of wedding stationery, websites and wording.

The guest list

Here a few points you'll need to consider when preparing to send out your invitations.

There are several ways that you can set out the guests for your day, with attendance numbers varying wildly from event to event. Some like to be surrounded by hundreds of their friends and families, whilst others prefer to share their day with only their nearest and dearest.

The process of making a guest list can be a long and laborious one. You'll find that you're constantly adding and subtracting names, sometimes from one day to the next. However, if you're securing a caterer for the reception it's important to get the numbers correct in order to ensure that everyone is fed!

There are a few considerations you'll need to allow for when drawing up your guest list. The size and capacity of the venue for the ceremony and reception is a good guide for planning guest numbers. If you have a venue with a capacity of 100 guests there's no point mapping out a guest list that's two or three times that. Similarly, if you've an intimate guest list of 60 you can rule out the larger venues – not only will this cost more, but you're guests will be rattling around the room!

As a rule the costs of a wedding can be linked to the number of guests – obviously the choices you make for the reception, catering and entertainment will have an impact, but as a basic rule the larger the number of guests you're catering for, the larger the bill! Many brides on a budget soon begin to cut the 'surplus' names from their list when they begin to add up the per-head cost for each guest.

Getting the numbers to fit is certainly not an easy job, but it's important to remember that you can invite guests to different elements of the day.

Laura's Bride Guide

The guest list can often be a point of stress for couples. Weddings are (for the most part) family occasions, and different family members will have different expectations of who should be on the guest list. To avoid any drama when the invitations have been sent out, chat to both sides of the family to find out if there are any expectations regarding the guest list. Whilst this doesn't mean that you have to invite your distant great aunty over your childhood best friend if space is limited, it does mean that you can discuss this with the relevant people – and, hopefully, avoid any offence!

Ceremony guests

These guests will attend the wedding ceremony – though it's customary for the invitations for these guests to be extended throughout the reception and the evening entertainments. However, if you have elderly or frail relatives, and friends with extremely young children, they may prefer to only attend the ceremony. But, rather than just assuming this, it'd be advisable to invite them to the entire event, and perhaps discuss with them face-to-face how they feel about staying until the evening.

Reception guests

These guests arrive at the reception venue after the marriage ceremony, where it is customary that a meal – either a traditional sit-down menu or something more informal – will be served.

Evening guests

With many celebrations lasting into the evening, there's the option of inviting an additional selection of guests for the entertainments of the later part of the event. This is an ideal way to include your wider circle of friends and co-workers.

Child-friendly or child-free?

Children can – and will – alter the tone of a wedding. Some couples see this as a mood-lightening, fun addition to the day, while others view it as a disruption to their sophisticated event. Everyone will have their own view on this, and the question of extending the invitations to children or not is often a touchy point for many soon-to-be-brides and grooms. This is something that only you will be able to decide, and you'll need to ensure that you make all your guests fully aware of your decision. Remember, for your guests with very young children, attending a wedding without them can be impossible, and you might be running the risk of some of your guests not being able to attend. If you love the thought of children brightening your celebrations, be sure to check that the venue is going to be able to accommodate prams, highchairs and baby changing.

If your decision is not to include children in your celebrations, do be sure that your guests are fully aware of this. While they might not see any issue with bringing along their little one on the big day, this will certainly have an impact on the reception, with staff having to find seating and food for all the additional guests – no matter how small!

The gift list registry

Use these hints and tips to get your wedding gift list down on paper.

Traditionally a wedding gift list was where the couple would write down the items they needed for their new life together. However, modern couples are often in a position of having cohabited before they take the step of getting married, which means that a list packed with toasters, cutlery sets and crockery can seem a little redundant.

If you aren't a cohabiting couple, then making your list might be a little more straightforward – many high street and online retailers will operate a Wedding Gift List service, allowing you to add a selection of desired items. The store will manage this as your guests make their purchases from your chosen items.

The question of cash

Your guests will want to mark your nuptials with a gift, but if you aren't having a traditional gift list then asking for money isn't the end of the world. To be sensitive to those guests that aren't familiar with this more modern concept, experiment with the wording of your request. Why not try, 'Help us celebrate our marriage with a donation to our Honeymoon Fund'; or perhaps include a couple of options for gift cards: 'Our first task as Mr & Mrs is to redecorate our home – we'd be grateful for any financial assistance towards this or Gift Cards to our favourite DIY store.'

Giving thanks

Couples will often receive gifts in the run-up to the wedding, either from guests that aren't able to attend or those who prefer not to bring the item on the day – which is common if it's something particularly sentimental or valuable. If you've used an online or high street gift service the items are usually dispatched or collection arranged after the wedding. Start a list of the items you've received alongside the names of the senders, or keep the tags or cards with the respective gifts to help make writing the 'Thank You' notes after the wedding a stress-free process.

'Save The Date' cards

Create wedding date cards with these four easy-make designs.

Sending out 'Save The Date' cards is a great way to get your wedding date saved in people's minds and diaries. This is a particularly good idea if you're planning far in advance, or for midweek weddings, since it allows guests the time to make arrangements for travel, time off work and accommodation. These cards simply need to notify guests of your wedding date – you can fill them in on the specific details, like place and time, on the invitation that'll follow.

Vintage luggage tag

- 5 minutes per tag
- £ Under £1 per tag

Collect supplies
- ❏ Luggage tag
- ❏ Stamping ink
- ❏ Alphabet rubber stamp set
- ❏ Black marker pen
- ❏ Distressing ink
- ❏ Scrap paper
- ❏ Pencil
- ❏ Ruler

Write the names
Crumple the scrap paper and press on to the distressing ink. Use the crumpled paper to dab on to the surface of the tag. Run the edges of the tag across the inkpad to stain.

With the black marker pen, write your names along the centre of the tag – sketch it lightly in pencil first to help to keep the letters neat.

Stamp on the details
With the alphabet rubber stamp set, pick out the letters and add 'Save Our Date' to the upper section of the card, and the date of your wedding below the

names. Draw pencil lines to act as a guide and work slowly to ensure neat placement of the text.

Finish the tags
Once all the ink has dried, carefully erase the pencil lines. The tags can be slipped into envelopes and sent out or hand-delivered to your guests.

Mini card

- Up to 10 minutes per card
- £ Under £1 per card

Collect supplies
- ❏ Light pink card 9cm x 12cm
- ❏ Scrap of dark pink card 5cm x 8cm
- ❏ Names and wedding date printed on cream linen paper
- ❏ Narrow ribbon 5cm
- ❏ Paper glue

Create the motif
Using your fingertips, carefully rip along three sides of the dark pink card – this will create a delicate frayed border. Repeat to

add the frayed border to the printed name panel, leaving both the left-hand sides of the card and printed paper un-ripped.

Secure the motif
Score along the centre of the light pink card and carefully fold in half. Position the printed paper on top of the dark pink card. Align the straight

edges and glue in place. Position the motif 1cm from the left-hand edge of the card and glue into position.

Finish with ribbon
Apply glue to the back of the ribbon and secure in place over the straight edges of the motif. Ensure the raw edges of the ribbon are tucked under and tightly secured. Write a personal message in the card and send to your loved ones.

Thumbprint key ring

- Up to 10 minutes per key ring
- £ Under £1.50 per key ring

Collect supplies
- ❏ Transparent key ring blank
- ❏ Coloured card 7cm x 7cm
- ❏ Thin ribbon 24cm
- ❏ Coloured marker pens with various tip sizes
- ❏ Fine-tip black pen
- ❏ Stamping ink

Write your message

Measuring the internal section of the key ring blank, cut two squares from cardboard 2mm smaller on all sides to fit neatly inside. Using the coloured marker pen write your names and upcoming wedding date on one piece of card. Sketch out lightly in pencil first for neatness. Vary the size of marker pen tip for contrast when inking in and create a border with dots and dashes.

Add thumbprint

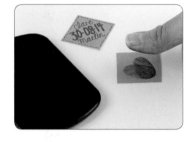

Create a heart shape by layering both of your thumbprints. Using the coloured marker create a border of dots and dashes. Place the two pieces of card with blank sides together and slip inside the key ring blank.

Finish with a bow

Secure the front of the key ring blank in place and tie a neat bow with the ribbon through the loop of the key chain to finish.

◀ Practise making a love heart shape with your two thumbprints a few times to get the layout right before you start on your project. If his hands are a lot larger than yours, use your thumb and his index finger for a closer size match!

Tying the knot card

- 20 minutes per card
- £ Under £2 per card

Collect supplies
- ❏ Pearlescent card blank 7.6cm x 7.6cm
- ❏ Thin card 7cm x 7cm
- ❏ Sharp pin
- ❏ Needle and embroidery thread
- ❏ Scraps of brown paper
- ❏ Black marker pen
- ❏ Pencil
- ❏ Tape
- ❏ Paper glue

Create the stitching motif

Working on the inside of the front of the card blank, draw a knot shape in pencil on the centre of the card. Use the sharp pin to create stitching holes evenly spaced across the drawn line – place on a soft mat to protect surfaces or your fingertips.

Stitch the motif

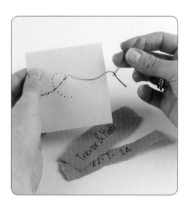

Thread the needle and begin stitching through the marked holes, following the loop direction of the knot. Once the motif has been stitched, trim the thread ends and secure with tape. Glue the thin card over the stitching to hide the back of the work.

Add the details

Tear two small strips from the brown paper and neatly write your names and upcoming wedding date. Place one at the top of the card and one at the bottom and glue into position.

Wording the invitation

Create your perfect cards with this guide to wording wedding invitations.

What you put in the invitation might seem trivial, but this is often the first taste your guests will get of the style for the wedding, not to mention the all-important information about the venue, dates and times.

Taking the traditional path

More formal and traditional invitations are sent out from the parents of either the bride, or the groom, or both, depending on who is 'hosting' the wedding:

> *Mr & Mrs Barton*
> *Request the pleasure of your company at the wedding of their daughter*
> *Miss Rebecca Barton & Mr Michael Burrows*
> *At The Chapel on The Green*
> *At 12 noon*
> *On Saturday the 16th August 2014*
> *Reception will follow at the Golf Club, Colchester*
> *RSVP*

> *Mr & Mrs Barton together with Mr & Mrs Burrows*
> *Request the honour of your presence at the wedding of*
> *Rebecca Barton & Michael Burrows*
> *At 12 noon at The Chapel on The Green*
> *On Saturday the 16th August 2014*
> *Reception will follow at the Golf Club, Colchester*
> *RSVP*

Making it modern

With the ever-changing face of family life, some brides and grooms prefer to make a more direct invitation from themselves to their guests. This also allows for the use of more relaxed language, which will be more fitting for informal events.

> *Jenny Cruickshank & James Coomber*
> *Together with their families*
> *Request the honour of your company at their wedding*
> *At The Old Town Hall*
> *On Saturday 27th April 2014*
> *RSVP*

> *Jenny Cruickshank & James Coomber*
> *Would like to invite you to their wedding*
> *At The Old Town Hall*
> *On Saturday 27th April 2014*
> *RSVP*

How you decide to word your invitation is all down to personal preference, but be sure to include all the essential information for the day – use the checklist below as a guide:

❑ Name of the bride (including surname if the bride's parents are not presented as the hosts).
❑ Name of groom (including surname if the groom's parents are not presented as the hosts).
❑ Name of hosts (can be presented as the bride's or groom's parents, family member or the couple themselves).
❑ Venue for the ceremony.
❑ Date – including day, month and year – and time of the ceremony.
❑ Location of the wedding reception – or indication that the reception follows on at the same venue as the ceremony, with details of the end time of the event.
❑ RSVP instructions – adding a date for RSVP will help you to keep on top of this.

You may also want to include...
❑ Information about your gift registry.
❑ Directions and local accommodation.
❑ Any specific dress code.
❑ Whether the invitation is extended to children.

Laura's Bride Guide

If you're printing the wording for the invitations from your home computer there are a number of stylish fonts you can use. Typography is an elegant skill that many designers work with in order to create really standout designs. However, with a little practice you can use a couple of tricks of the trade to give your own invitations the wow factor.

Consider mixing and matching fonts – this has a really dramatic effect and can be used to create both traditional and contemporary designs. There are a few simple rules that'll help you to achieve a professional look when using different typefaces. Try to mix serif with sans serif fonts; look for fonts with letters that have similar proportions; and don't go too crazy with the number of fonts you use – too many will look messy.

Once you've typed out the wording in a word processing document on your computer, begin by adjusting the alignment – moving the text to the centre or justifying it across the line. Look over the text, and add spacing and line breaks to give the words room to breathe. Use the font size and the bold function to add a highlight to the key words – your names, the dates, in fact anything that you really want to jump off the page.

Invitations

Wow your guests with a handmade wedding invitation. Here are four designs to try.

Depending on the number of guests you're hoping will attend your wedding the process of making your own cards can seem like a large task. Don't let that put you off! Begin by picking the style of card you want to make – use the ideas below, or adapt them to suit your personal style – and start out by making one single card. This'll help you to master the techniques used. To speed up the process, break the cards down into stages: if there are elements that need to be cut out do this first – get all the different components ready to use, and work in a production-line style.

Heart cluster card

- 🕐 10 minutes per card
- £ Under £2 per card

Collect supplies

- ❏ Natural card blank 14.8cm x 14.8cm
- ❏ Two pages from old unwanted book
- ❏ Black pen
- ❏ Letter stencil
- ❏ Ampersand rubber stamp motif
- ❏ 'Love' token motif
- ❏ Luggage tag
- ❏ Raffia ribbon
- ❏ Paper glue
- ❏ Heart templates

▶ As a bookworm I don't like to think of ripping up books! Rather than tearing apart one of your favourites, hunt out an aged-looking tome from a charity shop.

Add the antiqued paper

Tear a strip 4cm longer than the card blank and affix to the left-hand side of the card with paper glue, folding the ends neatly inside the card. Cut two large and two small hearts from the

remaining book paper and, layering the small one on the larger one, glue into position on the right-hand side of the card.

Create the tag

Tear a thin strip of book paper 2cm longer than the width of the luggage tag, and glue into position around the end of the card. Affix the 'love' token motif on top, at a slight

angle. Tie a small length of raffia ribbon through the luggage tag and glue into position on the card front.

Add the final details

Using the stencil set and black pen, neatly write your initials on each of the book paper hearts. With the ampersand motif rubber stamp and black ink, stamp the motif on to the card overlapping the book paper hearts. Try adding a heart motif and some wording to the envelope for the perfect finishing touch.

Haynes DIY Wedding Manual Exclusive

Contemporary designed wedding stationery is often at the top a bride's wish list, but if your budget doesn't stretch to commissioning a designer to create these, why not make you own with the help of a DIY website?

For my wedding stationery I used the website *downloadandprint.com*. Paying a subscription fee gives you 12 months' access to a whole range of different templates for invitations, RSVP cards, 'Thank You' cards and many more. This *exclusive* design is free for you to download and customise with your own text and information.

To get started, or to view the entire range, visit *www.downloadandprint.com/diytemplates/*.

Contemporary flat card

🕐 5 minutes per card
£ Under £2 per card

Collect supplies
- ❏ Dark brown card 11cm x 16cm
- ❏ Light blue card 10cm x 15cm
- ❏ Invitation printed out on cream paper 9cm x 13cm
- ❏ Paper glue
- ❏ Length of blue organza ribbon

Create the border
Secure the light blue card on top of the dark brown card, aligning the light blue card carefully to ensure there's a neat and even border on all sides.

Affix the wording
With the wording of your invitation printed out in your chosen font, colour and size, trim to 9cm by 13cm. Position carefully over the top of the blue card and stick in place. The border around the printed wording will be slightly wider at the top and bottom of the card compared to the two sides.

Embellish with a bow
Wrap the organza ribbon around the width of the card and tie in a neat bow. Smooth the sides and ends of the ribbon flat before slipping into an envelope.

▶ Fits into a standard 6cm x 11cm envelope.

Envelope sleeve card

🕐 15 minutes per card
£ Under £3 per card

Collect supplies
- ❏ Decorative handmade paper 10cmx 20cm
- ❏ Coordinating backing card 7.5cm x 10.5cm
- ❏ Invitation wording printed on to cream linen paper 6cm x 8cm
- ❏ Pencil
- ❏ Ruler
- ❏ Paper glue
- ❏ Paper scissors

Create envelope sleeve
Aligning the two short edges, fold the paper in half. Score 1cm along each of the two long sides and fold over. With the envelope folded in half, snip away a triangle at each side of the fold.

Secure the envelope
Cut away one folded edge on each side of one half of the envelope. Press the two folds in on the other half and work a line of glue along each. Fold the upper half over and press to secure – the two folded edges will be tucked inside and will secure the envelope.

Create the invitation card
Carefully draw a small semi-circle in the centre of the envelope opening and cut out. Align the invitation of the wording to the backing card and using the paper glue neatly secure in place and slide inside the envelope.

▶ Draw around the top of a glue stick to create a really neat curve.

Doily gatefold card

🕐 Up to 10 minutes per card

£ Under £2 per card

Collect supplies

❏ Cream gatefold A6 card blank
❏ Printed doily 18cm diameter
❏ Two large pink brads 2.5cm diameter
❏ Coordinating organza ribbon 20cm
❏ Paper glue
❏ Small hole punch

Secure the doily

With the doily positioned face down, centre the back of the gatefold card over it and fold the excess doily around the card. Remove the card and apply glue to the card back before pressing down to secure the doily.

Create the tie holes

Apply a small amount of glue to the edging of the doily and press the sides over the two side of the gatefold card – press the upper and lower section into the inside of the card. Using the small hole punch, create two holes on the front of the card, centred and 1.5cm from the outer edge of each gatefold.

Did you know?

A brad is like giant decorative split pin; the prongs are separated and bent back to secure it in place. You'll find these in the scrapbooking and cardmaking sections of craft stores.

Secure the brads

Push one brad through the hole on the right-hand side of the card and fasten in place. Press the prongs of the other brad through the end of the organza ribbon before securing through the card. Affix or write your chosen wording to the inside of the card and wind the ties around the two brads to close.

▶ Why not add a small offcut of the doily to the corner of the envelope with a small dab of glue before addressing and putting it in the post?

Ribbon tip

Ribbons are a pretty way to add quick and stylish embellishment to wedding projects. When working with ribbons it's essential to secure the ends to prevent them fraying and looking untidy. Here are a few quick tips for neatening the ends:

Cut at an angle

Using sharp fabric scissors, trim the end of the ribbon at an angle across the width.

Heat seal

With the ribbon end trimmed straight across, quickly pass the end of the ribbon through the flame of a candle. Aim to let only 1–2mm of ribbon pass through the flame. Be careful not to set the ribbon alight, and ensure the melted ribbon has fully cooled before touching it.

Swallowtail

Fold the ribbon in half, aligning the two long sides. Using sharp fabric scissors, position the blade on the fold with the tip angled towards the outer edge and carefully snip. When the ribbon is unfolded a neat 'V' shape – or swallowtail – will have been created.

Enclosures

To convey essential information to your guests, try one of these simple and stylish designs.

Not only will guests need to know the date and time of your wedding, they'll also need to know how to get to the venues – for both the ceremony and the reception – and out-of-town guests might need a list of local accommodation, or guidance regarding car parks. If you're having a gift list you'll also need to ensure your guests know where it's held.
Including enclosures with your invitations is a great way to present all the required information to your guests.

RSVP postcard

🕐 10 minutes per card
£ Under 50p per card

Collect supplies
- ❏ Natural card 7cm x 10cm
- ❏ Red and blue marker pens
- ❏ Black fine-tip marker pen
- ❏ Pencil
- ❏ Ruler
- ❏ Rubber alphabet set
- ❏ Stamping ink
- ❏ Letter stencil

Draw lines
Using the pencil and ruler draw a 5mm border around each side of the card. Holding the ruler at an angle mark out diagonal lines within the border.

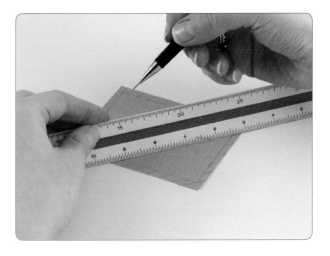

Add lettering
Using the stencil, mark out 'RSVP' on the upper section of the card – draft out in pencil, then work over using the fine-tip marker pen. With the alphabet set and black ink, add in the additional wording to the card.

Finish with a border
Working with alternate red and blue marker pens, colour in the diagonal panels within the border. When the ink is fully dry, carefully erase all pencil lines.

▶ The back of the card is left blank for you to fill out your postal address and add a stamp. Repeat the red and blue border if you fancy it!

Map motif directions card

- Under 10 minutes per card
- £ Under 50p per card

Collect supplies
- ❏ Print out or photocopy of old map trimmed to 9cm x 11.5cm
- ❏ Dark card 9.5cm x 12.5cm
- ❏ Details of wedding and reception venues printed on cream linen paper and trimmed neatly
- ❏ Vintage brown distressing ink
- ❏ Paper glue

Distress the paper

Taking each piece of paper with the details printed on, carefully run the edges along the surface of the distressing ink. This will give each piece an antiqued appearance and help it to stand out on the background.

Position the information

Once the distressing ink has fully dried, position the different elements of information around the card. When you're happy with the placement, secure into position with a dab of paper glue.

Mount the design

Position the map motif on the front of the dark card, creating a neat and even border around the motif. Once happy with the position, secure in place with paper glue.

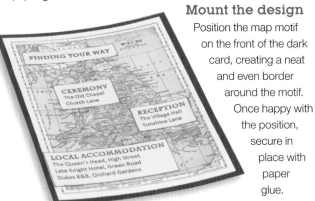

▶ Free, printable maps are available online and can be scaled to your required size. Alternatively, photocopy a map of the location of your wedding. This'll be particularly helpful for out-of-town guests.

Doily gift list card

- 10 minutes per card
- £ Under £2 per card

Collect supplies
- ❏ Coloured doily 14cm diameter
- ❏ Coordinated card 6.4cm x 7cm
- ❏ Gift details printed on linen paper in chosen font and trimmed to 4cm x 6cm
- ❏ Thin ribbon 45cm
- ❏ Vintage pink distressing ink
- ❏ Paper glue

Fold the doily

Place the card in the centre of the doily and fold the sides in over it. Repeat to fold the upper and lower sections over the card. Make a double fold to each of the side sections, reposition the card and fold the edges over to create a border. Use paper glue to secure into position.

Add the printed motif

Using the distressing ink, run each side of the printed element across the pad to add a touch of colour to the paper. With paper glue, position on to the centre of the card, overlapping the doily edges, and secure in place.

Create a ribbon tie

Find the centre of the ribbon, apply a dab of glue and secure into position on the back of the folded doily. Fold the upper and lower sections over and secure the ribbons in a bow at the front.

▶ When the card is closed with a neat bow it resembles a gift, which will remind guests to look over your gift registry!

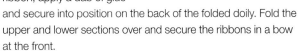

Guest options reply card

🕐 10 minutes per card
£ Under £2 per card

Collect supplies

❏ Pearlescent card blank 7.6cm x 7.6cm
❏ Strip of striped paper
❏ Coordinating print paper
❏ Fine-tip markers in coordinating colours
❏ Template
❏ Glue
❏ Pencil and eraser

Cut the template

Using the template provided, draw around the shape and carefully cut out the motif.

Draw a border

Using the marker pens, begin by drawing a solid border around the edge of the motif and then work around the inside to create a dotted border. Mark out your chosen words in the centre in pencil before inking over with the marker pen.

Complete the card

Using the glue, secure the strip of striped paper across the front of the card. Once dry, affix the motif to the front, carefully centring it before securing it into position.

▶ Insert a handwritten or printed sheet with the options for your guests. Let them know they simply need to indicate their preferences and send it back to you.

Wedding quick tip

If you aren't already blessed with the perfect strokes of fine hand lettering you can always learn a quick calligraphy cheat that'll add flair to your stationery:

Draw guidelines

Use a pencil to draw guidelines – create equidistant lines for a base line, a centre line and a top line. Make these lines an equal distance apart to help with neat positioning of your letters.

Write out the wording

Using neat cursive handwriting, write out your wording. Use the guidelines to create letters of even height and spacing. The letter should sit on the base line, with ascenders (t, h, l) reaching the upper and descenders (y, j, p) the lower lines.

Erase the lines

Carefully, ensuring that all the ink is dry, erase all the guidelines.

Add shaping to the letters

Add shaping to the letter by working the pen back over any lines formed by the down stroke, ensuring that these highlighted lines run smoothly into each letter shape.

▶ For a more a more dramatic look add in thicker shaping lines and flourishes.

▶ Mix and match calligraphy and neat block capitals for a modern look.

Wedding websites

Even the most tech-shy bride can use the Internet in the planning of her special day.

Aside from searching for venues, caterers and attire, couples can use the Internet to communicate information of their wedding plans and to keep guests up-to-date with all the developments. Depending on your time and computer skills, there are several options when it comes to getting online:

Start a blog

There are numerous free blog hosting sites that allow you to create your own blog, which you can update diary-style with new information about your wedding – you might want to set this as a running commentary, sharing the items that you make for your wedding or adding updates that'll supply your guests with information about the Big Day.

This is a great way to ensure that your guests feel part of the planning – and you might find that sharing your planning online will open you up to offers of help from friends and family, or even hints and tips from the wider community of brides online.

If you already have a blog you can add a wedding section, encouraging guests to visit with regular updates. Or, set up a new blog dedicated to your wedding. Many blogs have interactive features such as comments sections or polls – use these to get help with tricky decisions, or to find out information about your guests.

Laura's Bride Guide

There are many useful resources for the modern and cash-savvy bride on the Internet. There's a huge community of brides online, so visiting wedding forums is a great way to find answers to questions, to discover solutions to tricky wedding-related problems and even to make new friends.

▲ Discover more about Laura's handmade wedding plus lots more craft ideas, inspiration and how-to guides on her creative lifestyle website **www.madepeachy.com**

Why not try?

Here are some fantastic free blog hosting sites:

- Wordpress
- Blogspot
- Blogger

Search online for a selection of handy tips and tutorials to get your wedding blog under way.

Ready-to-go websites

There are a number of website-in-a-box style packages that you can buy, so even folks with little or no Internet experience can create their own websites. You can set up as many pages as you like – include information about your venue, how to get there, local accommodation, taxi and transport information. You could even include a page with information about how you met, or perhaps the proposal – this is great for getting guests in the wedding mood!

Some of us folks love to write, while others dread the thought of putting pen to paper – or fingers to keyboard – but the great thing about having your own website is you can do exactly what you want. You can upload lots of images, if you prefer, so if you'd rather not feel like you're back in the classroom writing essays simply make it a more visual website.

Stag parties and hen nights

It's customary to wave goodbye to single life with a celebration with friends and family.

The idea of stag and hen nights has evolved over the years, from a few humble drinks at the local pub to lavish trips abroad, pamper packages, and even week-long celebrations.

Stag parties

It's common for the stag night to be arranged by the best man. There has become something of a trend for playing pranks on the groom-to-be, but the acceptability of this really depends on the social group of your fiancé. For this reason that stag nights are held in advance of the wedding. Here are a few ideas for the menfolk:

Activity day
If the groom is passionate about a sport or activity, arrange a day that focuses around that – either plan to watch a sporting event or take part in one. Try your hand at golf, paintballing, or even hire kayaks and take to a local river.

Themed party
Getting kitted out for a fancy dress party is a lot of fun, not to mention perfect for capturing fun photos with your friends. Why not kit yourselves up as gangsters, superheroes or even movie characters?

Classic pub-crawl
A bar will often feature in the stag night plans. Arranging a bar crawl, with a pre-decided route, beginning at a venue that serves food and progressing to a nightclub, will enable a wide selection of guests to feel welcome – your dad or future father-in-law may not be keen to watch you strutting your stuff on the dance floor, but may join you for a drink earlier in the evening.

Hen nights

There's no better opportunity than a hen night to get together with your female friends and family and have a good knees-up. Some brides aren't keen on being decked out in 'L' plates and made to wear a net curtain veil. The chief bridesmaid usually helps with the preparations, and no doubt a word in her ear about things you love and hate about hen nights will set you on the path for a wonderful evening. Here are some ideas for the ladies:

Pamper day
Many spas and health clubs offer special packages for brides and their friends, which is the ideal opportunity to get a massage, sip some champers and relax with your nearest and dearest.

Take a workshop
Many craft shops offer party bookings for workshops. This could be the ideal opportunity to spend time with your friends while trying out a new crafting technique – there are lots of wedding-themed workshops for you to try!

Girls' night out
If you've already dusted off your dancing shoes then why not arrange an evening at your favourite nightspot? Planning to meet for evening cocktails or dinner first will encourage parents and other relatives to join the celebrations.

Stag parties and hen night checklists

However you celebrate your 'last night of freedom', be sure to run through this checklist to keep it on the right track:

- If your event is being planned as a surprise by a member of the bridal party, let them know in advance your budget and things you like or dislike.
- Set a budget – this lets you see what styles of celebration you can afford, and ensures that the costs for your guests are kept reasonable.
- Create a guest list. These pre-wedding events are also a fantastic opportunity for families and friends to get to know each other before the main event.
- Pick an event that encourages all of your chosen guests to come. Start the event earlier in a restaurant or cafe and have additional plans for the evening, to encourage more guests to attend the elements that they feel most comfortable with.

- Confirm your plans with any venues. It's a sad fact that some out-of-control parties have tainted the stag and hen night concept to a wide range of venues, with many refusing entry to large groups. Avoid disappointment by ringing ahead to your chosen venues – the manager will welcome the tip-off and may make a special fuss of you and your group.
- Stagger the dates of the stag and hen nights. Many couples do this so that either the cost of the events can be spread or the couples can balance their other responsibilities and wedding planning.
- Hold the parties in advance of the date. Despite being considered as a 'last night of freedom', aim to hold your parties a month or two ahead of your wedding. This will ensure that if anyone overindulges it won't ruin the wedding day.

Chapter 3 ·······································

The venue

The location of your special day is important. Here you'll discover how to find the perfect venue and learn a few clever DIY tricks to create fabulous decorations that'll suit your style and budget!

Choosing your wedding venue

With a little research and some careful consideration you'll find the wedding venue that suits your dreams and budget.

Picking the wedding location takes away a huge amount of pressure in the planning stages. Not only will you have found the venue, but you'll also have set a date that suits both your preferences and the location's availability. In many ways the venue for your wedding and reception set the tone of the wedding itself – for instance, if you've set your heart on a ceremony at a small country chapel, with a reception at the local village hall, you'll be hard-pushed to accommodate an 800-strong guest list. Similarly, if you book a wedding package at a castle, and you've decided on an intimate celebration with family and close friends, you might feel as though you're rattling around in there!

Essentially there are two types of marriage ceremonies: religious and civil, with civil partnerships for same sex couples constituting a third type of union. Which you choose will ascertain the style of venue that you'll require. Religious marriages are, as the name suggests, held at places of worship, and the arrangements for these are made directly with the officiant of the specific church.

Civil marriages can be held in any of a number of licensed venues, a list of which is held at the local Register Office (or 'Registry Office', as many people refer to it). Civil partnerships, like civil marriages, aren't permitted in places of worship, but there are a number of venues across the country that are registered for such ceremonies.

www.kerriemitchell.co.uk

Laura's Bride Guide

If you're looking to plan a wedding further afield – perhaps in your childhood hometown, or the place you first met – you might find the distance makes it tricky for arranging the various elements. Therefore it's crucial to build up a good relationship with the wedding coordinator or a dedicated person at the venue, who'll be able to give you assistance with local wedding suppliers.

What to ask when visiting a wedding venue

Here are a few questions you should ask while visiting a prospective wedding venue – of course, if you've something special and unique in mind for part of your wedding celebration, be sure to ask about that too!

- What is the capacity?
- Is the venue able to accommodate a ceremony and a reception? Are there any recommended reception venues in the locality?
- Is there overnight accommodation on site or recommended nearby?
- If the venue can hold the ceremony and reception, is there a bar or a will we/the caterer require a licence?
- Is there a wedding coordinator or a member of staff that we can liaise with during planning and the run-up to the wedding?
- Is there suitable provision for the elderly, disabled and children?
- Will the use of the venue be exclusive or will there be other guests, or even other wedding parties? (This is useful to know if you're booking at a large hotel or country club.)
- What is the cost for hire and what does that figure include?
- Is the premises licensed for live music?
- What time does the reception need to end?
- In multiple room venues, how many rooms will there be access to on the day? It's often good to have a quieter space for people to relax in if the dancing gets too much!
- Find out when the hire period runs from – are you able to get into the venue the day before to add your own decorations?
- What is the policy on clearing the venue following the wedding? Is there a set time the following day by which the venue needs to be restored to its normal state?

Outdoor weddings

If you love the countryside, consider making your vows in the great outdoors.

Under UK law civil ceremonies must be carried out in a licensed venue, and unfortunately this doesn't cover all of the great outdoors! If a building has a licence for civil ceremonies it doesn't automatically mean the grounds will too, so check with each venue to avoid any confusion. Some venues offer garden rooms, or conservatories or marquees to hold ceremonies. This is a great way of capturing the vitality of the outdoors without having to worry about the weather.

Increasingly there are wedding venues around the country that specialise in outdoor weddings. These often-rural locations frequently feature converted barns or arbours or some other roofed structure that's been specially created in order to be licensed for civil weddings.

Alternative options

If you're unable to find an outdoor wedding venue that fully meets your expectations and requirements, there is an alternative. Couples also have the option of splitting their wedding into its legal and ceremonial components. There are a number of companies that are dedicated to weddings of this nature, and will be able to assist in hosting a wedding ceremony outside in any location, although the ceremony won't be legally binding or recognised by law. In these instances, the couples arrange a legal marriage at a Register Office and then follow this with a marriage ceremony at their chosen venue. Couples are therefore able to have the legally binding wedding, perhaps with just their close family members, at the Register Office in the morning and then travel on to their chosen location to have a full wedding ceremony. Before ruling anything out, discuss your ideas with a specialist company to see if your wishes can be made into a reality.

Wedding day transport

Depending on the location of your wedding ceremony and reception, you'll need to get yourself there – in style!

While wedding transport will commonly get the groom and best man to the venue as well – although they usually arrive first (often in time for a beer in the local pub!) – the main consideration is getting the bride and bridal party to the ceremony. Of course, you might simply want to jump in a cab, but even if you're having a city wedding, don't leave anything to chance – make an advance booking with a taxi company, and be sure to let them know the booking is for a wedding, as no doubt they'll then ensure that the car – or cars – are suitably clean and tidy for the occasion. The transport you pick will also depend on the distance that you'll be travelling, the style of your wedding and the budget.

Horse and carriage

Nothing says romance like a horse-drawn carriage, and arriving at your wedding destination in true Cinderella style will certainly be memorable. Consider the distance to the venue and check it has suitable access when booking. Also, it's wise to consider how suitable the carriage is in rainy weather.

Vintage cars

There are numerous hire companies that offer a range of classic cars, so whether you fancy arriving like a Bond Girl or driving off into the sunset like the Lady of the Estate in a vintage Rolls-Royce, the options are endless. Plus, most hire companies ensure their drivers are dressed for the occasion, which will make you feel like royalty.

Custom camper vans

A classic camper van, with its polished chrome and colourful paintwork, will add a unique twist to your arrival. Companies specialising in hiring camper vans for weddings not only have a collection of models and colours for you to choose from, but have drivers that are passionate about their vehicles, ensuring your journey to the chapel is a memorable one.

www.dreambus-hereford.com

www.theredbus.co.uk

Routemaster bus

For couples that want to include as many of their bridal party and wedding guests as possible, hiring a specially restored Routemaster bus is the ideal option. The iconic red buses will be decorated with all the required trimmings and polished to a glistening shine – perfect for escorting you and your merry band of guests to the celebrations.

What to ask when arranging wedding transportation

- ■ What is the hire fee and hire period?
- ■ Is there time allocated for photo opportunities?
- ■ How many staff or drivers will there be and what are they like?
- ■ Is it possible to arrange multiple trips or collections from multiple locations to accommodate the bridal party?
- ■ Is there a limit or preferred distance to the venue?
- ■ Are you able to add or request ribbons or decorations to the vehicle – or can you request no decorations on the vehicle?
- ■ How will they ensure you get to the wedding on time?
- ■ Is the vehicle suitable for all weather conditions, and if not then what provision is made for rainy days?

Laura's Bride Guide

Depending on the location of your chosen wedding venue, you might be able to skip the cost altogether! As our wedding venue was within walking distance my husband-to-be and his best man decided to make the short trip on their BMX bikes, while I decided to take a leisurely stroll through the picturesque town with my Dad. If you intend to ditch the wedding cars and walk, cycle, or even ride your own pony, have a back-up plan just in case. Ask friends or guests with lovely or unique cars to make sure they're clean and shining (and vacuumed free from dog hair) to act as a stand-in on the day, should the heavens open!

www.kerriemitchell.co.uk

Flower arrangements

Try your hand at floral arrangements with these four quick-make designs.

Weddings and flowers go hand-in-hand. The style of flower you pick is down to personal preference, but remember that exotic or out-of-season blooms will be more expensive. There's a wide range of elegant silk and foam flowers that can be bought from florist supply stores and craft shops alike – these are a great way to add non-wilting floral decorations.

Gerberas in vintage glass bottles

- 🕐 10 minutes per trio
- £ Under £10 per trio

Collect supplies
- ❏ Gerberas with long stems
- ❏ Floristry wire
- ❏ Secateurs
- ❏ Vintage glass bottles

Trim the stems
Using the bottles as a guide, use the secateurs to trim the flowers to a suitable length – the larger the bottle, the longer the stem. Ensure that the cut is made diagonally across the stem to assist with water absorption.

Wire-wrap the stems
Starting directly underneath the bloom, circle the wire a couple of times around the top of the stem. Continue carefully wrapping the wire in a spiral down the length of the stem and secure at the bottom. Wrap the wire so that it grips the stem, but not so tight that it damages it.

Insert into bottles
Fill the bottles two-thirds full with fresh water and insert one stem into each bottle. The wire can be gently manipulated to ensure that the blooms are facing in the preferred direction.

Country jug flowers

- 🕐 Under 10 minutes per jug
- £ Under £10 per jug

Collect supplies
- ❏ Small vintage-style jug
- ❏ Stocks
- ❏ Thistles
- ❏ Secateurs
- ❏ 2m natural twine

Neaten and trim
Using the jug as a gauge, trim each stem to the desired length, allowing the stocks to stand around 5cm taller than the thistles. Working along the length, trim off any excess foliage to neaten – work gradually to ensure you don't remove too much.

Arrange in the vase
Fill the jug two-thirds with fresh water and begin to place the longer stocks at the back and the thistles towards the front. Before adding each new flower, snip the end of the stem to create a diagonal cut to aid water absorption.

Neaten and add string accent
Move the arrangement around within the jug until you're happy with it. Wrap the natural twine around the neck of the jug three for four times and tie in a neat bow at the front.

▶ If your arrangement won't hold its shape, slip a handful of glass beads or marbles into the bottom of the jug and reposition the flowers. The beads help to prevent the ends of the stems from slipping in the vase and unbalancing your arrangement.

Tulips in gel beads

⏱ Under 15 minutes per vase, plus time to hydrate gel beads
£ Under £10 per vase

Collect supplies
- ❏ Mid-sized bunch of tulips
- ❏ Secateurs
- ❏ Lengths of pink and orange organza ribbon
- ❏ Aqua gel beads
- ❏ Circular vase

Trim and neaten stems

Remove the lower leaves and, using the vase as a guide, trim to correct length, cutting the stems at an angle to aid water absorption. Try to vary the height of the stems, with larger ones at the back and sides and slightly shorter ones at the centre and front.

Create the arrangement

Pour the pre-soaked gel beads into the vase and begin inserting the stems. The gel beads will hold the stems securely whilst you finalise the design.

Add an accent ribbon

Holding the ribbon double, wrap it around the centre of the vase. Knot to secure and tie in a neat bow.

▶ Gel beads are available in a wide range of colours and shapes from floristry stores. These beads need to be soaked in water for up to 24 hours to rehydrate to full size. They don't supply a huge amount of water to the flowers, so to prevent wilting top the arrangement up with fresh water.

Foam flowers in gift box

⏱ Under 15 minutes per box
£ Under £10 per box

Collect supplies
- ❏ Foam roses in pink and white
- ❏ Cardboard gift box
- ❏ 6cm wide pink velvet ribbon
- ❏ 1.5cm wide white grosgrain ribbon
- ❏ Hot glue

Embellish the gift box

Position the wide pink ribbon 2cm from the bottom of the box and use the strong glue to affix it. Secure the grosgrain ribbon to the upper section of the velvet ribbon and neaten and overlap the ends at the back of the box.

Insert blooms

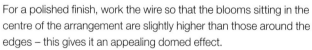

Insert the foam roses into the opening in the gift box. Bend and manipulate the wire stems to ensure that the flowers sit neatly in the box.

Complete the design

Adjust the placement of the flowers as required.

For a polished finish, work the wire so that the blooms sitting in the centre of the arrangement are slightly higher than those around the edges – this gives it an appealing domed effect.

Fabric bunting

Lengths of lovely printed cotton bunting are a fantastic decorative addition to a wedding venue.

Combine a few basic supplies and simple sewing skills to create colourful bunting that'll add a fun party feel to wedding venues and outdoor areas alike. Select a mixture of prints in different designs and shades for an eclectic vintage style or use a refined palette for a more sophisticated look.

Collect supplies
- ❏ Selection of printed cotton fabric remnants
- ❏ Ribbon, at least 4m, 20mm wide
- ❏ Scissors
- ❏ Rotary cutter
- ❏ Ruler
- ❏ Pencil
- ❏ Card or paper

Make a template
Draw a template for the pennant on card and cut out. The template that I've made measures 18cm along the flat base, 22cm down the centre line from the base to the tip, and the two long sides measure 22.5cm.

Calculating bunting lengths

To make the bunting described here, every 3m length of ribbon will provide up to nine pennants. Decide on the length of strand you want to make and cut the required number of flags to suit. Leave up to 40cm pennant-free at the start and end of each strand to create ties.

Cut the fabrics
With the fabrics folded in half and half again, place the template on to the material and use the ruler and rotary cutter to slice the shape. You'll be able to cut up to six layers of fabric with your rotary cutter. Flip the template each time to get the most economical use of the fabric.

Sew a pennant
Place two cut pennants right sides together, aligning the raw edges, and pin in place. Select a straight machine stitch and, taking a ¼in seam allowance, sew along one long edge to the point. Stop the machine to pivot the work, then sew back up the other side, leaving the base unstitched to turn through.

Quick tip

You can sew all the pennants one after another, or you can create a chain effect by allowing the machine to run on a few stitches between finishing one flag and starting the next. Continue until all the flags have been stitched and you'll end up with a string of flags. Snip the thread chain between each to separate, then go on to create the bunting.

Turn the pennant to the right side

Snip away the excess fabric at the point of each flag and turn through to the right side. You might need to use the end of the pencil to ease the tip of the flag out. Press the flag – sliding the card template inside as you press will help you to get neat, crisp seams.

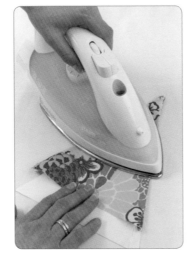

Create the ties

Fold the length of ribbon in half, aligning the long edges. With a straight stitch and working close to the two open edges, sew the length of ribbon together for at least 40cm. This is repeated at the end of the length of flags and will make hanging the bunting easier.

Laura's Bride Guide

We decorated our wedding venue with lashings of bunting, and received many wonderful compliments on it throughout the day. After measuring the beams of the wedding venue to calculate the amounts of bunting I'd need to sew, I did feel rather daunted at the prospect. However, by setting up a 'production line', first cutting then stitching and finally joining, I was really pleased with how quickly this whole project was created.

Assemble the bunting

Place the first pennant so that it's sandwiched between the ribbon and stitch across. Stitch the ribbon together to create the space between the flags. I like to leave a gap the same size as the width of a single pennant, but this can be as big or small as you like. Position the next flag between the ribbon and stitch in place. Continue until you've incorporated all the flags and finish by sewing 40cm of ribbon at the end to make the second tie.

Fancy flags

Use the rounded template in the same way as the triangle. Sewing together two pieces with right sides facing and using a 6mm seam allowance, clip around the curve before turning though and pressing. These rounded flags can be stitched into place just like the triangular type – or you can mix and match the two different styles!

Chapter 4

The bride and bridesmaids

Picking your wedding attire is no doubt an exciting experience. It can also be a costly one, especially if you've a troupe of bridesmaids to frock as well – add into the mix a flower girl and this might be enough to tip you over the edge. Here are a few secrets to help ensure that your unique style is present on your wedding day.

Your wedding gown

Get the dress of your dreams without blowing the budget.

The range of wedding dress styles available is as wide and varied as the brides themselves. Some brides already know what style, shape or design of dress they want, which leaves them with the job of just finding it at a price to suit their budget. Alternatively, as is often the case, the bride might have no idea what to wear! So here are some of the options to consider when searching for your perfect dress.

Designer dress

Probably the most coveted of all is the couture wedding gown, although with the hefty price tag that often goes along with it many brides refuse to visit boutiques for fear of falling in love with something they can't afford. If a designer dress is a top priority you may be able to shuffle your budget around to accommodate it – you might have to spend less on accessories and shoes, for instance.

Before heading to a designer boutique armed with your cheque book and grim resolve that you're about to blow the budget on a vision of lace and tulle, find out if there are any sample sales or end-of-season sales at local stores. Styles that are sometimes a few months old might now be considered as 'old season' and could have a substantial discount.

Many boutiques even sell off the sample dresses that have been used for brides to try on, and are consequently considered 'shop soiled' – but don't let that expression put you off: such a dress will be given star treatment in cleaning and repairs before you buy it, so it'll look fabulous on your wedding day.

Vintage dress

Whether you search through vintage clothing fairs, or try and strike it lucky at a second-hand shop or a jumble sale, a vintage dress is often excellent value for money.

The appeal of wearing a vintage gown is growing in popularity with brides. As the garment will be sold as seen in many cases, be sure to check any fastenings, seams and hems are in good condition – or can be easily repaired or replaced. If you aren't keen on sewing, take along a stitching enthusiast, as they'll be able to help you to ascertain if any necessary repairs or adjustments are possible.

www.kerriemitchell.co.uk

Heirloom dress

Perhaps one of the most sentimental dresses you could wear is a wedding dress that belonged to a family member or a close friend. A dress that's been passed down to you can always be modified, modernised, customised and tailored to your exact body shape, either by yourself or with the assistance of a skilled dressmaker.

Pre-loved dress

Don't be put off by second-hand dresses – these can be exceptional value for money. What's more, they'll have only been worn for a few hours, and will have been deeply cherished by the bride on her wedding day, so it's an excellent way to snap up a bargain. As with vintage dresses, they will be sold as seen, so with private sales ask the seller for an honest report of the condition and, if necessary, pictures of the hemline, fastenings and seams.

High street dress

As more brides are refusing to compromise on style and price, many high street stores are increasing or launching ranges of wedding dresses. Not only are these affordable, but as they're ready to wear off-the-peg they're also ideal if you've a short timescale to work to. Although such ready-to-wear gowns don't come with the custom fitting of a bespoke wedding dress, there's no reason why you can't take it to a seamstress or a professional dressmaker and have any required alterations made to ensure the perfect fit. If you're planning on anything other than the taking in of seams or shortening of hemlines and are considering more drastic alterations, perhaps to the neckline or sleeves, be sure to discuss fully with your chosen seamstress in advance to avoid any disappointment.

Handmade dress

If you're looking for something entirely unique for your wedding day, you can recruit the services of a professional dressmaker who'll be able to transform your initial ideas into sketches and then transform those into your dream wedding dress. Or, you might fancy digging out your sewing machine (or asking a skilled family member or friend), grabbing a dress pattern and sewing your own dress. Ensure you allow enough time to make the dress – rushing to finish can lead to unfortunate mistakes. Make a toile (a version of your dress in a cheaper fabric or calico) first; this will give you a practice run, allowing you to perfect techniques and make adjustments before you begin cutting your wonderful – and no doubt expensive – wedding dress fabric.

Spend wisely

Whatever you choose to spend on your wedding dress it'll no doubt be one of the most expensive garments you purchase. As with buying any high-value item, be sure you're making a safe transaction. Reputable bridal retailers will clearly explain the order process, the amount required for the deposit and when the instalments or final payments are due. Dressmakers may also request a percentage of money in advance, usually to secure the work and cover the cost of materials, with the balance being paid at final fitting or collection. If you're purchasing online always be sure the transaction is a safe one; with online auction sites and private sales, request making payment on collection, or if shopping overseas take advantage of an escrow facility (a secure means of transferring funds via a 'middle-man').

Full-length veils

Create and customise your own veil with these four elegant designs.

Wedding veils can cost hundreds of pounds, and whilst these intricate and exquisite adornments are wonderful, if you're working to a budget it can be hard to find the funds to indulge. A two-tier veil can be made quickly and easily at home with a few simple supplies.

The veil

- 🕐 Under 1 hour
- 💷 Under £20

Collect supplies

- ❏ Ivory tulle 270cm wide x desired length
- ❏ Thin ribbon 20cm
- ❏ Clear hair comb
- ❏ Coordinating thread
- ❏ Sharp dressmaking shears
- ❏ Tailor's chalk
- ❏ Strong glue

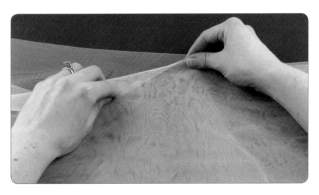

Fold the veiling

Working on a large table, or very clean floor, fold the tulle across the length of the material (this will probably be the way that it was folded when you purchased it). Fold the fabric in half again at the middle point and align the short ends.

Trim the veiling

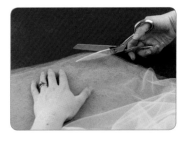

If you need to make any alterations to the length trim away the excess fabric now. Position the folded layers of fabric with the long edge towards you and the other, shorter folded edges to your left-hand side (you may want to reverse this if you are left-handed). Using tailor's chalk draw a neat curve along the raw edges and cut away the unfolded corner.

Create the tiers

Unfold the veiling completely, to reveal a large rectangle with rounded corners. Take one end of the tulle and fold it over to create a shorter tier. As this tier will be worn over the face for a portion of the day, stand in front of a mirror to test the length, refold until you are happy with the lengths of both tiers. Mark this fold line with tailor's chalk.

Gather the tulle

Thread a needle with a length of coordinating cotton and knot the end. Using long gathering stitches, work across the veiling 0.5cm under the chalk line. Once one line of gather stitches has been worked, don't fasten the thread – rethread the needle with a second length of cotton and repeat to work a second line of stitches across the tulle 0.5cm above the first.

Draw up and fasten

Holding the two loose ends of thread, begin pulling them to draw them through the material and gather up the tulle. Using the hair comb as a guide, continue pulling the threads until the gathered section is the same width as the comb. Thread both of the ends of cotton through the needle and fasten with a few small neat stitches and a secure knot.

Ribbon-wrap the comb

Add a dab of glue to the back of the hair comb and secure one end of the ribbon in place. Wrap the upper section of the hair comb by bringing the ribbon over the top and down through the teeth. Continue until the entire length is wrapped. Secure the end with a dab of glue. Once the glue has dried, open the veiling out, placing the gathered section on the ribbon-covered portion of the comb.

Secure to the comb

Thread a needle with cotton, align both ends of the cotton and knot securely so that the thread is doubled. Begin stitching in place. Work in neat stitches around the upper section of the comb and between the teeth, before passing through the gathered section and passing it back over the comb. Work back and fourth a couple of times to ensure the veil is secure and fasten with a neat knot on the back of the comb to finish.

▶ The best way to calculate the amount of tulle required is to measure from the crown of your head, or where you intend to position the veil, to the floor (or desired length if you require a shorter veil); adding to this the amount for the upper tier – measuring from the crown to where you want the tier to end – will give you more than enough tulle for a full and luscious veil. The typical lengths of veil are shoulder-length (45–60cm), fingertip-length (95–100cm), floor-length (152–182cm) and cathedral-length (exceeding 255cm).

Silk flower embellishments

⏱ Up to 20 minutes to embellish
💷 From £5 per veil

Collect supplies
☐ Four wired-stem silk roses
☐ Needle and coordinating thread
☐ Jewellery wire cutters
☐ Completed veil

Wrap the wire on to the comb

Open the two tiers of the veiling out and, beginning at one end of the gathered section, feed the wire through the veiling and twist carefully around the teeth of the comb. Press the wire ends in towards the comb, snip away any excess wire and press-in any sharp ends. Repeat to secure the remaining blooms across the gathered section over the comb.

Sew to secure

Thread the needle with cotton and knot the two ends together so that the thread is doubled. Working from the underneath to the top of the veil, pass the needle through the tulle, catching the flowers with a neat stitch. Work back and forth across the comb ensuring that all the roses are stitched securely.

Fasten off the thread

With the thread to the back of the veil, work a couple of small neat stitches though the tulle and secure with a small knot. Snip the thread ends to finish.

Sparkle accents

🕐 Up to 40 minutes
💷 From £10 per embellished veil

Collect supplies
- ❏ Needle and coordinating thread
- ❏ Metal-backed diamanté sew-on gems
- ❏ Crystal beads
- ❏ Hot-fix crystals
- ❏ Hot-fix tool
- ❏ Brown paper
- ❏ Completed veil

Secure the hot-fix gems

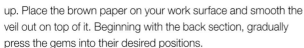

Set the hot-fix tool to heat up. Place the brown paper on your work surface and smooth the veil out on top of it. Beginning with the back section, gradually press the gems into their desired positions.

As the front section of the veil is worn both down over the face and swept back, many brides want the gems to be visible on both sides. To do this, work on one side first to secure the gems, ensuring that they aren't positioned too closely together over your face. Once secured, flip the veil over and secure a second gem directly to the back of the first. When adding gems try slipping on the veil intermittently, to check that you're happy with the position and progress.

▶ Test applying hot-fit gems on an offcut of veiling. Don't press the hot tip of the tool on to the material, as it will melt or scorch it!

Secure the sew-on gems

Thread the needle with the coordinating thread and knot the two ends together so that the thread is doubled. Open the veiling out and begin at one end of the gathered section. Feed the needle through the veiling, then through the holes on the back of the gem and stitch securely in place.

Add crystal beads to finish

Repeat the process to secure the remaining crystal beads across the gathered section of veiling across the comb. Knot the threads securely on the underside of the veil and trim the thread ends.

Pearl-trim edging

🕐 From 3 hours per full-length veil
💷 From £20 per veil

Collect supplies
- ❏ Coordinating edging, long enough to accommodate the entire veil edge plus 5cm
- ❏ Needle and coordinating thread
- ❏ Pins
- ❏ Completed veil

Pin the edging in place

Open out the veil and lay it flat on a clean work surface. Starting at the comb on one side of the veil, work around the outer edge with the trimming and carefully pin in place. Leave 2cm of trimming extra at each end of the pinned line.

Stitch in place

Thread the needle with coordinating thread and begin working around the outer edge of the veiling to stitch the trimming into place – pass the needle around the edge of the veiling, catching the trimming and holding it in place. Use the mesh holes on the tulle as a guide to keeping the stitching straight and neat, and ensure that the trimming is secure to the veiling with each stitch.

Neaten the ends

Once the length of trimming has been stitched in place, turn the veil so that the underside is uppermost. Pin the 2cm of unstitched trimming in towards the comb. Using small neat stitches, carefully secure the trimming to the underneath of the veil to conceal it. Knot the thread and trim away thread and trimming ends.

Birdcage veils

Create your perfect birdcage veil, with four styles to choose from.

While some brides feel self-conscious wearing a grand, full-length veil, a more compact design can be equally stunning and is perfectly suited to vintage-style wedding dresses and themes.

Vintage-style birdcage veil

- ⏱ Under 40 minutes
- £ Under £10 per veil

Collect supplies
- ❑ Russian veiling 30cm x 60cm
- ❑ Needle and coordinating thread
- ❑ Ribbon
- ❑ Hair comb
- ❑ Sharp dressmaker's scissors
- ❑ Strong glue

Trim the veiling

Fold the veiling in half along its width, aligning the two shorter edges. Using the dressmaking scissors, carefully snip away the edges on one corner opposite the fold – this cut edge will become the inside edge of the veil and will help to give it shape.

Gather the veil

Thread the needle with a length of coordinating thread and work across the inside edge of the veiling, starting at one angled corner and ending at the other, weaving in and out through the mesh. Don't fasten off the thread – repeat to add a second line of gathers and carefully draw up to the width of the comb before securing with a firm knot.

Secure the ribbon to the comb

Add a dab of strong glue to the back of the comb and wrap the ribbon around the upper section of the comb, taking it over the top and between the teeth until the entire comb is covered. Secure with a dab of glue.

Attach the veiling

Position the gathered veiling on top of the comb and, using the coordinating thread and needle, carefully secure it to the comb. Secure the threads with a tight knot on the underside and snip away the thread ends.

Feather embellishments

⏱ Under 40 minutes
£ Under £15

Collect supplies
❏ Russian veiling 30cm x 60cm
❏ Needle and coordinating thread
❏ Ribbon
❏ Hair comb
❏ Sharp dressmaker's scissors
❏ Strong glue
❏ Diamanté buttons or brooch
❏ Feather

Trim and gather the veiling

Fold the veiling in half along its width, aligning the two shorter edges. Using the dressmaker's scissors, carefully snip away the edges on one corner opposite the fold. Thread the needle with a length of coordinating thread and work across the inside edge of the veiling, starting at one angled corner and ending at the other. Don't fasten off the thread, repeat to add a second line of gathers and carefully draw up to the width of the comb before securing with a firm knot. Secure to the comb with neat hand stitches.

Add the feather

Position the feather on the veil, with the plumage to the back. Arrange until you're happy with the placement and secure in position with a dab of glue. Set aside to dry fully.

Add the diamanté button

Position the diamanté button over the end of the feather. Using a needle and coordinating thread, work small neat stitches through the button, catching the feather at the same time to secure it in place. Knot on the underside and trim the thread ends.

Veiled hat base

⏱ Under 40 minutes
£ Under £20

Collect supplies
❏ Russian veiling 30cm x 60cm
❏ Needle and coordinating thread
❏ Teardrop untrimmed hat base
❏ Hair comb
❏ Selection of flat-backed rose cabochons, beads or gems
❏ Sharp dressmaker's scissors
❏ Strong glue

Trim and gather the veiling

Fold the veiling in half along its width, aligning the two shorter edges. Using the dressmaker's scissors, carefully snip away the edges on one corner opposite the fold. Thread the needle with a length of coordinating thread and work across the inside edge of the veiling, starting at one angled corner and ending at the other. Don't fasten off the thread, repeat to add a second line of gathers and carefully draw up to the width of the comb before securing with a firm knot. Position the veiling to the side of the hat base and secure in place with small stitches using the needle and coordinating thread.

Add the embellishments

Position the decorative beads, gems or cabochons along the veiling and fix in place with a few dabs of strong glue (some cabochons are drilled, allowing you to stitch them into position).

Affix the comb

Place the comb in the desired position on the underside of the hat base and, using the needle and coordinating thread, carefully stitch in place with a few stitches across the comb. Fasten the threads with a tight knot on the underside and snip away the thread ends.

Brighten with coloured ribbons

⏱ Under 40 minutes
£ Under £10 per veil

Collect supplies
❑ Fine tulle veiling 30cm x 60cm
❑ Needle and coordinating thread
❑ Hair comb
❑ Sharp dressmaker's scissors
❑ Strong glue
❑ Ribbon
❑ Decorative ribbon
❑ Diamanté ribbon sliders, one large and one small

Trim and gather the veiling
Fold the tulle in half along its width, aligning the two shorter edges. Using the dressmaker's scissors, carefully snip away the edges on one corner opposite the fold. Make a series of small folds across the length of the tulle to create a neat pleated section in the centre on the trimmed edge. With a needle and coordinating thread, carefully secure the folds in place with a few neat stitches.

Add the ribbon accent
Thread the small diamanté slider on to the narrower ribbon, and then place on top of the wider ribbon before feeding through the second slider. The smaller slider will sit in the centre of the larger one. Secure in place with a dab of strong glue.

Laura's Bride Guide
With a birdcage veil, you can wear the comb with the teeth positioned towards the veil or away from the veil, depending on your hair type and hairstyle. Try out the comb positioned in you hair in both directions before you decide which way to secure the veiling.

Secure to the comb
Using the needle and thread, carefully secure the gathered tulle to the comb by working the stitches over the back of the comb and between the teeth. Work back over the length of the comb until it's fully secured and fasten off.

Complete with the embellishments
Place the ribbon embellishments centrally over the comb and glue securely into position. Fold the ends of the ribbon to the back and glue to secure.

▶ This veil is made using tulle instead of Russian veiling. Check out the range of different styles and colours of veiling materials in your local fabric store.

Hair accessories

These four ideas will help you add some additional glamour to your bridal party.

Hats are a key feature at weddings – many guests love the opportunity to wear a fancy accessory. These designs for hats and fascinators utilise simple millinery techniques that are easy to try at home.

Pearl and sparkle tiara

- From 3 hours
- £ Under £20

Collect supplies
- ❏ Tiara band
- ❏ Silver-plated 0.80mm wire 6m
- ❏ Four small white pearl beads
- ❏ 14 small rose pink pearl beads
- ❏ 12 clear crystal beads
- ❏ 17 pink crystal beads
- ❏ Flat-nosed jewellery pliers
- ❏ Jewellery pliers
- ❏ Jewellery wire cutters

Secure gems to lengths of wire

Cut a 15cm length of wire, slide a pink pearl on to the centre and fold the wire in half. Hold each end firmly with the round nose jewellery pliers. Rotating your hands in opposite directions to create a tight twist. Repeat to create four pink crystal, four clear crystal, two white pearl and two pink pearl 6cm wire twists in total.

Make the accent shapes

Using the same twisting technique, thread a pink pearl on to the centre of a 20cm piece of wire and create a 1cm twist. Add a clear crystal on one side of the wire and fold to create a 1cm branch and twist tightly. Repeat to add a sparkle on to the other side of the wire. Repeat to make an identical wire twist.

Make the centrepieces

The centrepiece is made more dramatic by layering two elements together, with the larger element at the back. Using the same twisting technique, place a pink pearl at the centre of a 30cm piece of wire and make a 1cm twist. Create a 1cm branch with a clear crystal then a second with a pearl directly below. Repeat on the second side.

Create the front centrepiece

Using the same twisting technique, place a pink pearl with a pink crystal either side of it to the centre of a 25cm piece of wire and create a 1cm twist. Add a silver crystal and twist for one 1cm, repeat to create a branch on the other side.

Layer the front elements

Place the smaller accented wire on top of the larger one, holding both the left-hand-side wires together with the jewellery pliers to create a tight twisted wire. Repeat to create a tight twisted wire on the right-hand side.

Safety tip

The ends of jewellery wire can be extremely sharp. Use a sewing thimble to protect the tip of your finger and goggles to protect your eyes when cutting wire.

Affix to the tiara band

Starting with the centrepiece, position the different elements around the band, ensuring the design is mirrored on each side. Set the centrepieces

highest, and decrease the height of the other embellishments as you work towards each outer edge. Twist the wires around the band to secure into place. Trim the excess and use the flat-nosed pliers to press securely to the band.

Add an accents wire to the headband

Thread the remaining ten pink pearls and nine pink crystals on to 30cm of wire, alternating between

the two. Beginning at one end of the design, create a 0.5cm tight wrap of wire around the tiara band. Continue wrapping around the band, feeding the wire in between the embellished wire and positioning a pearl or crystal at the front as you wrap. Continue across the band and finish by securing 0.5cm of tight-wrapped wire at the other end. Snip all excess wire and press all ends into the tiara with flat-nosed pliers.

Vintage brooch hair comb

- ⏱ Under 20 minutes
- 💷 From £5 per comb

Collect supplies

- ❏ Wire hair comb
- ❏ Vintage brooch
- ❏ Strong glue
- ❏ Coordinating ribbon
- ❏ Feathers
- ❏ Tapestry needle

Wrap the comb

Place one raw end of the ribbon flat on the back of the upper section of the comb and secure in place with a dab of strong glue. Position the feather at one end so it lies across the length of the comb and secure with a dab of glue. Allow to dry and begin wrapping the ribbon over the top of the comb and bringing it up between the teeth. Work back over the comb to create a double wrap.

Secure the ribbon

Snip the ribbon end at the back of the comb and thread on to the tapestry needle. Feed the needle through the wrapped ribbon at the back of the comb and secure the raw edge with a dab of strong glue.

Add the brooch

Once the glued ribbon has fully dried, open the clasp on the brooch and carefully push the pin

under some of the wraps of the ribbon at one end of the brooch. Close the clasp to secure. If the brooch is really large, heavy or very precious, use a coordinating thread and work a neat hand-stitch over the clasp to secure the brooch even more firmly into place.

▶ As brooches can easily be removed from the comb, this is a great way to wear a really beautiful brooch that might be something old or something borrowed, without wearing it pinned to your precious wedding gown.

Floral fascinator

⏱ Under 50 minutes
£ From £10 per hat

Collect supplies
❑ Untrimmed circular hat base
❑ Small corsage of artificial (raffia or silk) flowers
❑ 1m of brown Sinamay ribbon
❑ Clear hair comb
❑ Needle and thread

Create a ribbon embellishment
Hold one end of the Sinamay ribbon and fold into a loop. Fold over the other end to create a large figure of eight. Repeat to create a second, smaller figure of eight inside.

Secure to the hat base
Leaving one long tail of Sinamay ribbon hanging free, position to the side of the hat base with the loop overhanging the edges. Secure in place with neat hand stitches worked through the Sinamay ribbon and base.

Add the floral embellishment
Trim away any excess of wire at the bottom of the flower corsage and position in the centre of the ribbon embellishment. Secure in place with neat hand stitches through the base.

Affix the comb
Align the comb on the back of the hat base, with the prongs facing away from the design, and stitch in place, working through the previous stitches for a secure and discrete finish.

Feathered hair bow

⏱ Under 40 minutes
£ From £5

Collect supplies
❑ Burgundy crinoline 15cm wide x 110cm
❑ Headband
❑ Strong glue
❑ Needle and thread
❑ Accent feathers

Create a bow
Holding the end of the crinoline, create a small flat loop. Fold to make a second loop opposite it. Repeat to make two larger loops underneath the first two loops, leaving a short tail. Work a couple of small stitches in the centre to secure.

Add feathers
In turn, carefully glue the feathers to the centre of the bow. Each feather should be positioned so it stands proud of the top of the bow. Making each feather stand at a slightly different height will give a more striking finish. Hold firmly until the glue has fully dried.

Secure to the headband
Add strong glue to the upper surface of the headband on the side where the bow will be positioned. Press the bow in place and allow the glue to set. Add strong glue to both the centre front of the bow and the section of headband that lies directly behind it. Carefully wrap the tail of the crinoline around the centre of the bow to secure it firmly to the headband. Trim the excess and allow the glue to dry fully.

Hair and make-up

Every bride wants to look her best on her wedding day – use these budget-savvy beauty essentials, for stress-free style.

With all eyes on you, you'll want to look and feel your very best on your special day. That doesn't necessarily mean recruiting a team of stylists – there are a number of things you can do yourself to ensure that you look lovely on the Big Day!

There are many mobile beauticians that specialise in wedding-day packages. These usually offer a trial session before the date, which will allow you to talk through ideas for your look and the style of your dress and accessories, to achieve a complementary hair and make-up style. Have a look through some bridal or fashion magazines for ideas, but remember to think of these only as inspiration, since you'll need to be realistic – if your hair is currently in a close crop you'll find it hard to achieve flowing mermaid locks in six weeks, even with the help of hair extensions. Use your trial session to find the look you feel happy and comfortable with.

If you're confident applying your make-up and fixing your own hair there's nothing to say you can't take care of these yourself on your wedding morning. Have a practice run before, though, so you know how long the process takes, what supplies you'll need and check that the look lasts all day. Don't be too tempted to pile on lots of make-up in order to obtain a lasting finish – this'll give an unattractive caked appearance to your skin. You can always pack a mini-make-up bag to slip to a bridesmaid for necessary touch-ups later in the day. Use the products and routine you'd use for your everyday or 'night out' make-up, and keep the look fresh with a flattering and natural palette of eyeshadow and blush.

Wedding morning beauty regime

- Get a good night's sleep. Your wedding day, despite flying by, is actually a long event, and ensuring you're well rested will help you to stay fresh-faced on the day.
- Get manicure and pedicure in advance. With guests shaking your hands and admiring your wedding ring all day, you'll want your hands and nails to look their best. Either get a manicure a couple of days before the ceremony or shape and polish your nails yourself the evening before.
- Stay hydrated. Keeping your fluid levels topped up, both in the morning and throughout the day, will help you to feel and look revitalised.
- Eat breakfast. It's called the most important meal of the day for a reason – it gives you the kick-start of energy that you'll need to see you though the exciting first few hours of the day.
- Allow yourself extra time. Whether you're doing it yourself or getting a hair and make-up artist in, feeling rushed will not only make you feel stressed, it can also lead to making mistakes and will take more time in the long run.
- Don't be tempted to try out anything new on the day. You might be struck with the sudden urge to do something completely different to your hair, but unless you're really confident about the results you could be setting yourself up for a disaster.
- Relax and smile. No matter how confident you are, most brides will feel nervous at some point on their wedding day. Take a few deep breaths, feel yourself relax and smile, and you'll start to feel – and look – better in no time!

www.kerriemitchell.co.uk

Wedding garters

Garters are a huge part of wedding tradition and are considered a sign of good luck. Make your own from one of these four stylish designs.

Originally intended as a functional item to hold up stockings, these little undergarments are more about style than functionality at modern weddings. It's become symbolic for the groom to remove the bride's garter and toss it to a group of unmarried men at the wedding, although many brides keep them as a memento.

Broderie Anglaise garter

- 🕐 Under 2 hours
- 💷 From £5 per garter

Collect supplies
- ❏ Length of 2cm wide elastic 5–10cm shorter than thigh measurement
- ❏ Length of broderie anglaise 1½–2 times the length of thigh measurement
- ❏ 2cm wide satin bias tape same length as Broderie Anglaise
- ❏ Thin blue ribbon
- ❏ Needle and thread
- ❏ Pins
- ❏ Safety pin
- ❏ Tapestry needle or bodkin

Create the casing
Place the broderie anglaise with the wrong side facing uppermost on a flat surface, position the length of bias tape along its length with the folded parts innermost. Pin carefully in position and stitch in place using the fold lines as a guide.

Thread the elastic
With the safety pin attached to the end, thread the elastic through the casing, pushing the Broderie Anglaise into gathers, until the elastic is protruding from both ends. Overlap the ends of the elastic by 2.5cm and sew together with neat stitches to secure.

Add ribbon detail
Tuck under the raw edges of the ends of the Broderie Anglaise to the inside and neatly stitch together.

Starting at the front of the garter, begin weaving the blue ribbon though the lace holes in the centre of the Broderie Anglaise. Work around the back of the garter until you're back to the front. Pull the tails of the ribbon even and tie into a neat bow.

Rippled ribbon garter

- 🕐 Under 2 hours
- 💷 Under £5

Collect supplies
- ❏ 2cm wide elastic 5cm–10cm shorter than thigh measurement
- ❏ 5cm wide ivory satin ribbon 1½–2 times the length of thigh measurement
- ❏ 2cm wide satin bias tape same length as satin ribbon
- ❏ Ivory grosgrain ribbon 25cm
- ❏ Diamanté button
- ❏ Needle and thread
- ❏ Pins
- ❏ Safety pin

Create the casing
On a flat surface position the length of bias tape along the length of satin ribbon with the folded parts innermost. Pin carefully in position and stitch in place using the fold lines as a guide.

Thread the elastic
With the safety pin attached to the end, thread the elastic through the casing, pushing the ribbon into gathers, until the elastic is protruding from both ends. Overlap the ends of the elastic by 2.5cm and sew together with neat stitches to secure.

Add a diamanté accent
Tuck under the raw edges of the ends of the satin to the inside and neatly stitch together. Trim 5cm of grosgrain and set aside. Fold the remaining section into a loop, press flat and wrap the remaining 5cm of ribbon around the centre. Hold in place with a couple of small stitches. Pin the bow to the front of the garter and, with the diamanté button in place, sew to secure.

Rose motif tulle garter

- 🕐 Under 2 hours
- 💷 Under £10

Collect supplies
- ❏ Length of 2cm wide elastic 10cm shorter than thigh measurement
- ❏ Two lengths of 2cm wide satin bias tape 1½–2 times the length of thigh measurement
- ❏ 30cm x 70cm of rose tulle
- ❏ Needle and thread
- ❏ Pins

Create a casing
Open the bias tape out and pin together along one side with the right side facing. Use the fold lines as a guide for placing the pins and sew on the outer edge of

the bias tape. Fold the bias tape back together and join the second side along the two folds in the long edges using slip stitch.

Insert the elastic
Using the safety pin on the end of the elastic, feed the length through the centre of the casting until the elastic is protruding from both ends of the bias tube.

Overlap the ends of the elastic and sew securely together. Fold under the raw ends of the bias and stitch together.

Position the rose motifs
Arrange the fabric of the bias strip into neat gathers around the elastic. Working in short strips of rose tulle, begin to pin in

place. Pin one motif to the elastic, pull it under tension and pin again, allowing the fabric to lay flat against the taut elastic.

Secure into place
Once the strips have been pinned, sew in place with small hand stitches through the centre of each motif, ensuring that you hold the elastic under tension as you sew.

Velvet and tulle garter

- 🕐 Under 2 hours
- 💷 From £5

Collect supplies
- ❏ Length of 2cm wide elastic 10cm shorter than thigh measurement
- ❏ Length of 5cm wide velvet bias tape 1½–2 times the length of thigh measurement
- ❏ Strips of tulle 15cm x 200cm
- ❏ Needle and thread
- ❏ Pins

Create a casing
Fold the ribbon in half with the pile of the velvet outermost. Working over the edges, carefully stitch together to create a tube. With the safety pin on the end, push the

elastic through the velvet casing until both ends of elastic are protruding. Overlap the elastic by 2.5cm on each end and sew securely together. Even out the velvet around the elastic, tucking the raw edges inside and stitching together.

Gather the tulle
Fold the tulle in half, aligning the two short ends. With a needle and thread, work a line of long gather stitches along the centre of the tulle, leaving the thread unfastened at

the end. Repeat to create a second line of gather stitches. Pull the thread ends to gather up the tulle until it's the same width as the stretched garter band.

Secure the tulle
Pin one end of the gathered strips to the inside of the garter band and, with the band under tension, continue pinning until the entire length is secured. Work along the

inside of the garter band to stitch the tulle securely to it. Fasten the thread neatly to finish.

▶ If you're confident using a sewing machine, you'll be able to sew the long straight seams of these garters quickly and then finish the ends with neat hand-stitching.

Corsages

Offer female members of the bridal party a beautiful handmade corsage.

While fresh flower corsages are wonderful to wear, due to their colours and fragrances, they do need to be created just before the event in order to ensure they're as fresh as a daisy on the day. Here are some pretty ideas for fresh flowers and non-wilting crafty alternatives.

Gerbera corsage

🕐 15 minutes per corsage
£ From £3 per corsage

Collect supplies
- ❏ Two gerberas
- ❏ Two wide leaf foliage cuttings
- ❏ Gold organza ribbon
- ❏ Floristry tape
- ❏ Secateurs
- ❏ Corsage pin

Trim and create placement

Ensuring the flowers are well hydrated, trim the stems to 3cm below the bloom. Place the wide leaf cutting behind the two flowers and, when happy with the placement, trim the leaf stems to the same length.

Wrap the stems and attach the pin

Holding the arrangement securely, place the corsage pin on to the back of the corsage with the fastening facing outermost. Using a length of floristry tape, carefully begin wrapping the stems together tightly enough to hold the pin in position, cut the tape and allow the self-adhesive tape to secure the end.

Add a ribbon bow

Aligning the centre of the ribbon to the back of the corsage, wrap around the stems two or three times and return to the front to tie in a neat bow to finish.

Freesia corsages

🕐 15 minutes per corsage
£ From £3 per corsage

Collect supplies
- ❏ Two freesia blooms with leaves
- ❏ Secateurs
- ❏ Corsage pin
- ❏ Floristry tape
- ❏ Ric rac trimming

Trim and arrange the flowers

Using the secateurs, cut the stems to 2cm from the start of the flowers. Holding together with the foliage, trim the stems of the leaves to the same length.

Secure the arrangement

Position the blooms and leaves together in a downward cascade, with the stems pointing upwards. Position the corsage pin on to the back of the arrangement with the fastening outermost. Secure in place with wraps of floristry tape, allowing the self-adhesive ends to secure the wraps.

Add trimming to the stems

Place the cream ric rac trimming around the wrapped stems and criss-cross down the length before tying in a bow above the flowers.

Fresh flowers

Cut flowers are prone to wilting, so make your corsages either last thing the night before, or early on the morning of the wedding. Once made up into corsages you won't be able to water them, so ensure they're well hydrated before beginning, and once made store them in a cool place away from direct sunlight. Where possible select plants that are just about to bloom, like these freesias – they'll open on the day and look their best.

Foam rose corsage

🕐 Under 20 minutes
£ Under £3 per corsage

Collect supplies
❑ Three small foam roses
❑ Secateurs
❑ Pink ribbon organza
❑ Corsage pin
❑ Glue gun

Create a ribbon loop
Holding one end of the

ribbon, twist to create a loop. Twist again to make a second loop opposite to create a figure of eight. Repeat to create another figure of eight, so that you have four loops in total. Let the end of the ribbon hang down from the centre.

Trim and position the flowers
Using the secateurs, trim the wire stems of the roses to they're 3cm below the blooms. Position them as desired and twist the

stems together to secure. Position the looped ribbon behind the flower and glue to secure into the desired position.

Wrap the stems with ribbon
Once the glue has fully dried, position the corsage pin on to the back of the design and begin wrapping the ribbon around the stems to secure the pin in place. Wrap tightly and add a dab of glue to secure the end of the ribbon at the back of the corsage.

Felt bloom corsage

🕐 Under 20 minutes
£ Under £3 per corsage

Collect supplies
❑ Selection of felts in shades of pink and green
❑ Large pink brad
❑ Green grosgrain ribbon
❑ Corsage pin
❑ Hole punch
❑ Strong glue
❑ Template

Create the bloom
Using the template, cut out five petal shapes from the pink felts and two leaf shapes from the green felts. Arrange in a flower design and use the hole punch to make a hole in the centre and feed the felt shapes on to the brad.

Add the ribbon
Cut the ends of the ribbon into neat swallowtails and fold in half. Spread the ends of the ribbon slightly and use the hole punch to make a hole in the folded section. Feed on to the brad and secure on

the reverse. Position the pin on to the back of the corsage and secure with a dab of strong glue.

Complete the corsage
Once the glue has dried, place a strip of scrap felt over the back of the corsage pin, leaving only the fastening exposed, and affix in position with strong glue.

Bridal bouquet

Make your own unique bouquet with these four stylish designs.

Modern bridal bouquets come in all shapes and sizes, and can be a costly addition to the budget. Whether you prefer fresh or artificial, vintage or modern, these ideas can be easily created at home for a unique touch.

Felt heart and flower bouquet

🕐 Under 1 hour
£ Under £15

Collect supplies
❏ Selection of twigs between 15cm–30cm
❏ Five felt hearts
❏ Dark and light green felt
❏ Selection of pink, red and white felt
❏ Floristry tape
❏ Strong glue
❏ Template
❏ Needle and thread
❏ Natural twine

Cut the felt
Using the template, cut the felt into the leaf and petal shapes – the rounded shapes for the petals and the pointed for the leaves. You'll need two green pieces for each leaf and four pieces for each flower.

Glue the flower into position
Wrap the petals around the stick in turn, layering each one over the last. Secure each one with a dab of glue. Allow a small section of the felt to sit on the stick. Wrap base of the flower where it joins to the twig with floristry tape to neaten.

Secure the leaves into position
Using the same technique, layer the two components for each leaf into position and glue to secure to the twig. Neatly wrap the join between the felt and the stick with floristry tape.

Complete the bouquet
Work around the collection of twigs to add leaves to some, flowers to others, and secure the felt hearts to the remaining twigs using a generous amount of glue. Once all the components are fully dry create an arrangement and secure in place by wrapping a 3cm wide strip of light green felt around the middle section of the sticks. Secure the felt with glue before wrapping with twine and fastening in a bow.

Vintage brooch bouquet

- ⏱ Under 4 hours
- £ From £25

Collect supplies

- ❑ Selection of vintage brooches and diamanté buttons
- ❑ Floristry wires and tape
- ❑ 6cm wide ivory satin ribbon
- ❑ Two pairs of jewellery pliers
- ❑ Strong glue

Attach the brooches to wires

Hold the wire steady with one pair of jewellery pliers and use the second set to carefully wrap the wire around the tip of the first set. This will create a small loop. Continue until you have a tight coil of wire.

Secure the brooch to the wire

Open the brooch and feed the point through the coiled wire.
Fasten securely and twist the two pieces of wire together to hold the brooch in position. Press the wire coil tightly around the brooch pin to lock it into position.

Wrap the wires

Once all the brooches have been secured on lengths of twisted wire, begin at the top and wrap each one with a length of floristry wire. Working down and back up the length will give a neat finish and added strength.
Use the self-adhesive tape of the floristry wire to affix the end.

Arrange the bouquet

Gather together the wrapped wire broaches and arrange in your hands until you're pleased with the placement and bouquet arrangement. Secure together with a length of floristry tape and then use the wide ribbon to wrap the wired stems, carefully covering the base of the bouquet. Secure the raw ends of the ribbon at the back of the bouquet with a dab of strong glue and allow to dry fully. Secure the loose ends with another dab of strong glue.

▶ This bouquet can be as large or as small as you like – simply add in more wired brooches to create a larger bouquet.
You can pick up lots of pretty old pieces of costume jewellery from flea markets and charity shops. I've added in a selection of diamanté buttons to fill out the bouquet. Use jewellery pliers to press in any sharp points to prevent snagging your gown. Don't forget that this isn't a bouquet for tossing after the ceremony – it could cause someone an injury!

Hand-tied rose bouquet

- Under 30 minutes
- £ Under £20

Collect supplies

- ❏ Fresh roses
- ❏ Wide pink velvet ribbon
- ❏ Two pearl-head pins
- ❏ Secateurs
- ❏ Floristry tape

Strip and trim the stems

Working carefully around any thorns, remove the leaves from each rose stem. Trim the stems to equal 25cm–30cm lengths from the base of the bloom.

Twist the flowers into position

Taking each flower in turn, place the head of the rose next to the first and pass the stem over the front. Rotate the flowers in your hand to position the next flower, with the blooms touching, and again bring the stem over the previous one. Continue to rotate the bouquet adding more flowers, and the stems will form a neat twist. The rotation technique for adding in each flower should result in a neat cluster of blooms with the initial flower, in the centre, standing slightly proud of the remaining dome of flowers.

Secure the arrangement

View the bouquet from all angles to ensure that you're happy with the positioning. After any adjustments, secure in the middle of the stems with a strip of floristry tape. Use the wide velvet ribbon to wrap only the centre section of the stems, covering the floristry tape but leaving the upper and lower sections of the stems visible. Fold under the ends of the ribbon and pin in place, ensuring the tip of the pin is pushed back to the inside of the bouquet.

▶ As the ends of this bouquet are not wrapped you'll be able to store it in water before the day. Be sure to dry off the excess water before handling, to prevent getting watermarks on your wedding gown.

Silk peony bouquet

- Under 20 minutes
- £ Under £10

Collect supplies

- ❏ Selection of silk peonies with foliage
- ❏ Floristry tape
- ❏ Pink paper streamer
- ❏ Strong glue

Create the design

Ensuring that the stems are all of a similar length, hold the flowers in one hand and begin adding in more to create an arrangement. Twist each flower so that the foliage is pointing away from the centre of the bouquet. Silk flowers often have wire inside the stems – bend and manipulate this to get your desired placement.

Secure the bouquet

Once you're happy with the placement of all the flowers, use a length of floristry tape to hold securely in position. Allow the self-adhesive tape to secure the end.

Wrap the stems

Wrap the paper streamer up and down the length and over the base until all of the stems are completely secured and concealed. Secure the end of the streamer with a dab of glue and allow to dry fully.

▶ Artificial or silk flowers are often just as beautiful as the real thing, and they'll live on long past the wedding day! Take a look at the wide selection of styles at a floristry supplier to find the best option for you.

Wedding dress hanger

Personalise your own wedding dress hanger in three simple steps.

Wooden dress hangers are far prettier than the wire varieties, and are strong enough to hold even the heaviest, frothiest wedding gown. The section of wood can easily be embellished with name, date or sentiments for a unique keepsake.

Personalised wooden clothes hanger

⏱ Up to 20 minutes
£ From £3 per hanger

Collect supplies
❑ Wooden hanger
❑ Pyrography tool
❑ Hot glue gun
❑ Foam roses
❑ Ribbon
❑ 40cm white organza ribbon
❑ Pencil and eraser

Write on words and motif
Draft out the word 'Bride' or your name on the sides of the hanger and sketch a heart shape into the centre. With the pyrography tool heated to the correct temperature, and using the correct safety features, begin working over your pencil lines to heat-etch the design into the wood.

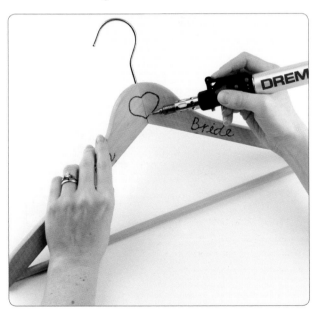

Twist on flowers
Position the foam roses in the desired position on the front of the hanger, using the wires to secure them to the hook section of the hanger. Twist tightly to secure into place. Use wire cutters or pliers to snip away any excess – be sure to fold in any wire ends to prevent them from snagging the fabric on your dress.

Add ribbon bow
Position a ribbon around the flowers, looping it securely around the hanger hook before trying into a pretty bow to hang down at the front.

▶ For safety, wear a heat-resistant glove when working with a pyrography tool. Fresh-cut flowers, whilst lovely, will wilt quickly on the day and could leak water or sap on to your wedding gown.

Flower girl dress

Create a custom ensemble for your flower girl with these easy-make ideas.

This pretty design can be made with just a few basic sewing skills – secured with tie straps, you'll not have to worry about adding any fiddly buttons or tricky zips. A couple of easy-make accessories really set off the dress in style!

Flower girl dress for ages 4–6 years

🕐 Under 6 hours
£ From £15

Collect supplies
- ❑ 2m of silk dupion in chosen colour
- ❑ Wide ribbon
- ❑ Pins
- ❑ Dressmaker's scissors
- ❑ Tailor's chalk
- ❑ Bodice pattern template

Cut the pattern
With the fabric folded in half, position the bodice piece on the fabric, aligning the fold and extending the lower section by 8.5cm. Using sharp dressmaker's scissors, cut the piece from the fabric four times, refolding the fabric to achieve the most economical placement. Two pieces form the front bodice and two form the back.

Line the bodice
Place two bodice pieces right sides together and pin in place. With a straight machine stitch and working with a 1cm seam allowance, join the

two pieces along the upper section and across the ties – leave the two side sections unjoined. Repeat to create the lined back bodice section. Turn through to the right side and press.

Create the bodice side

Open out the lined bodice section and position the second on top with right sides together. Align the side section of the bodice front with the bodice back, and the front and back linings, and pin in place.

Complete the bodice seams

Starting at the lower edge of main fabric work a 1cm seam along the length of the side of the bodice, and continue working across the lining section to finish the side seam. Repeat for the second side. Press the side seams open and push the lining into the inside and neatly press the bodice.

Gather the skirt
Cut a piece of fabric 51cm by 128cm for the skirt section. Along one of the longer edges, work two rows of gather stitches 1cm from the edge of the fabric, within the seam allowance. Do not fasten off the threads – pull them to begin gathering up the fabric across the stitched lines.

Join the skirt seam

Placing the skirt with right sides together and using a 1.5cm seam allowance, join the skirt together along the centre back seam, leaving 1.5cm at the

top of each seam un-stitched to allow for gathering. Press the seam open. Turn the skirt through to the right side and pull up the threads to adjust the gathers until the top of the skirt is the same width as the lower section of the bodice. Fasten the gathers by knotting the two threads.

Position the ribbon

Place the length of ribbon along the lower edge of the bodice, centre and pin in place. The right side of the ribbon should be facing outermost on the garment, and the unpinned edge should be facing towards the upper section of the bodice. Pin in place along the front of the dress.

Stitch the skirt in place

With the wrong side of the skirt outermost, slide over the bodice and, with the right sides of the skirt and bodice facing, align the raw edges of the bodice and the gathered skirt together and pin in place, ensuring the gathers of fabric are neatly distributed. Join together with a straight machine stitch.

Professional finish

I've worked the stitches in a contrasting colour, so as to show the positioning of the seams, but you'll need to colour match your threads and fabrics in natural light.

The ribbon should be caught securely in the seam on the front of the bodice only, allowing the free ends to be tied at the back of the bodice. The gather stitches should be secured inside the seam line and should not need to be removed.

Hem the skirt

Check the length of the skirt against your flower girl and pin the hem to the desired length. Work with either a line of hand or machine stitches to secure the lower hem. Press neatly and tie the ribbon in a bow at the back of the dress.

▶ This dress is self-lined so that the small ties at the shoulder have a neat finish. As this garment doesn't have lots of fussy fastenings, like buttons and zips, and because it only requires a small number of sewing techniques, it's simple enough for even the most novice dressmaker. Or, if you're more experienced, use this design as a basis for your own customisation and embellishments.

Flower girl posy

- Up to 30 minutes, including drying time
- £ Under £7 per posy

Collect supplies

- ❏ 6cm polystyrene ball
- ❏ Pack of small paper roses
- ❏ 20cm of woven pink ribbon
- ❏ Scissors
- ❏ Knitting needle or long skewer
- ❏ Hot glue

Create the hanging loop

Using the knitting needle or long skewer, carefully create a hole through the centre of the polystyrene ball. Double over the length of ribbon and feed through. Knot the two raw ends at the bottom of the ball.

Trim and secure blooms

With the scissors, carefully remove the heads of the artificial flowers from the stems, and working with one bloom at a time apply hot glue to the back of the flower and stick into position.

Complete ball

Continue covering the entire ball with the flower heads, ensuring that the flowers are close enough together so that the foam ball isn't visible. Allow all the glue to fully dry.

▶ To avoid any hazard to children, ensure that all small parts are securely glued into position.

Flower girl headband

- Under 15 minutes
- £ From £5 per headband

Collect supplies

- ❏ Length of 6cm wide pink velvet ribbon
- ❏ Two felt hearts
- ❏ Hairband
- ❏ Needle and thread
- ❏ Strong glue

Create a fixed bow

Cut a 30cm length of ribbon, fold the raw edges in to create a loop and secure together with a few neat hand stitches.

Secure to the headband

Place the half-finished bow on the headband and, using a needle and thread, carefully stitch it in place. If the hairband is plastic and not covered with webbing like this one, use a dab of strong glue to secure.

Complete the bow

With the remaining length of ribbon, wrap the stitched centre of the bow and secure with a dab of glue. Pass ribbon around the headband and secure on the underside with a few neat stitches. Position the felt hearts on the front of the bow, secure in place with a generous application of strong glue and allow to dry fully.

Mother of the bride

Assist the all-important mother of the bride in the wedding preparations.

The mother of the bride – and equally the mother of the groom – are often made quite a fuss of on the Big Day and are an important part of the bridal party.

Style guide

No doubt your mum will have her own sense of style, and might even have an idea of what she would like to wear for the occasion. Keeping her in the loop with your plans – colour schemes, the level of formality and the style of the venues – will help her to make an informed choice when selecting her outfit. Whether or not your future in-laws are already familiar or have only briefly met, be sure to keep both parties updated on colours and styles of possible garments to help them select the right dresses, and to avoid their outfits clashing or looking too closely matched.

The question of hats

Many women love an excuse to don a fancy hat, while others feel self-conscious in one. Traditionally hats were common in church weddings, where women respectfully kept their heads covered.

What about the Dads?

It might seem that we've forgotten about the menfolk, but this isn't the case. Unless your parents have wildly differing tastes, the father of the bride and the father of the groom will opt for colours that coordinate nicely with their partners – after all, they'll want to look their best too. If you've any unusual or unique dress codes – you'd like the men to sport bow ties, perhaps – be sure to give them some advance warning. You don't want your Dad hunting through his collection of dated ties at the very last minute!

However, in modern times it's just as common to see women attending a church wedding without a hat or a civil ceremony with a hat. Guests often consider the wearing of hats to be a sign of a very formal wedding, although increasingly guests are making their own decisions as to whether they wear one or not. Elegant fascinators are certainly a way to feel dressed-up without having to worry about looking dishevelled or requiring extra primping time between the ceremony and reception to rid themselves of 'hat hair'.

www.kerriemitchell.co.uk

Chapter 5 ···

The groom and groomsmen

The process of getting the groom and his merry band of groomsmen ready for the celebrations needn't be a headache. From buying or hiring suits to drafting out speeches, there's something here for every man. Plus, use a little creative know-how to add some wonderful finishing touches to the groom's special day attire.

···

Groom's suits

Get the right outfit for your husband-to-be and his tribe of groomsmen by following these handy tips.

In much the same way as brides' fashions, grooms are now taking to the chapel in a wide range of styles of garment, from kilts and dress shirts to cool linen casual suits – even teaming crisp shirts with denim jeans! Here are a few tips to help you through the maze of getting suited and booted.

Selecting your style

It's your wedding day, so of course you want to look your very best, but what you decide to wear is dependent on a number of factors. Whilst your bride might be secretive about her gown, there's no reason why you can't find out about the style to make sure that you make the perfect pair on the day. For example, if the dress and wedding style is very formal and traditional then a groom decked in a casual linen suit might seem out of place. Similarly, if you're planning a relaxed and laid-back affair, a morning suit with top hat, tailcoat and cravat might be rather odd.

Of course, the bride and groom don't have to match, far from it – if you've been discussing your chosen wedding theme and style for the day, you'll have a pretty good idea of whether you want to really go to town or simply want to keep it smart and stylish.

Finding the fit

Getting the right fit of suit isn't simply a case of trial and error. Following a few simple rules for your specific body type will save you from trying on countless ill-fitting suits.

Slim or shorter men should avoid long jackets that end towards the thigh – aim instead for a jacket that finishes at the top of the legs to create the appearance of more height and proportion to the upper body. Jackets that feature two or more buttons also create an appearance of height over a single buttoned jacket. For grooms concerned about their height, having trouser legs altered so they sit quite low over your shoes (without being so long they scuff the

www.kerriemitchell.co.uk

ground), and selecting shoes of a similar tone to the suit, will give the illusion of longer legs.

On the other hand, if you're extremely tall you might want to wear a suit that stops you from looking like a beanpole, in which case the principles outlined above should be reversed. Select a jacket that's wider and sits longer on your body, giving the upper body a more solid, balanced appearance. Opting for fitted or slightly tapered trousers cut to sit just over the ankle of the shoe also gives a more proportioned look.

If you're keen to add the appearance of bulk to your upper body, jackets with more features like pockets, or double-breasted designs, will draw the eye and make a feature of your torso. In contrast, if you want to reduce the appearance of your upper body size, select a design without these features for a more slimming effect.

The most important place to start is to get measured by a professional. Having your correct measurements makes finding the right suit less of a chore.

Made-to-measure

While a made-to-measure service is of course a luxury, if you're having trouble finding a suit to fit and flatter your frame in rental stores or high street shops, visiting a tailor is a fantastic way to get exactly what you want, and to your exact body shape. It's also important to remember that having a suit made for you will take longer than picking one up off the rack. In most cases, once you've had initial measurements taken and selected a suit design, you'll be required to attend a further fitting or two. This ensures the suit is made exactly right and allows for making any adjustments to the fit or even, where possible, the design. Getting your suit designs under way early will ensure you have enough time to get the suit handmade. Some tailors offer services for off-the-peg suits, which is a cheaper way to achieve a bespoke look.

Hiring a suit

When hiring a suit the process will be much the same; you'll begin by having your measurements taken, and once your size has been decided you'll be able to make your selection from a range of styles, fabrics and colours. For couples that are looking to accent the groom's wear with a coloured waistcoat and cravat, many hire shops will have a selection of popular colours to choose from. Depending on the hire company, once you've selected the size and style of your suits the order will be placed for your required date and will be secured with a deposit. The suits can either be collected or you can often make arrangements for them to be delivered to you a few days before the wedding – this is usually when you make the full payment. After your wedding, the suits will be collected or can be dropped off to the hire company ready to be laundered for the next wedding. As the suits will be given to you in excellent condition, you'll be expected to return them in a similar condition.
Of course, accidents do happen, and depending on the damage you may have a fee deducted from your deposit; the hire company will ensure you're fully aware of the charge process should this be the case.

Cufflinks

Formal shirts often require cufflinks. Make your own with these four unique designs.

With the female members of the bridal party being decked out in corsages and fascinators, make sure the menfolk don't feel left out with these simple and stylish cufflinks.

Wooden bow cufflinks

🕐 Under 10 minutes per pair
£ Under £5 per pair

Collect supplies
❏ Two 2cm wooden heart buttons
❏ Thin gold ribbon
❏ Cufflink blanks
❏ Hot glue

Create a bow
Thread the thin ribbon through the two holes in the heart-shaped buttons and knot on the front to secure. Tie the ends in a bow and neaten them with a diagonal cut.

Secure embellishments
Add a dab of glue to the knot, and snip and heat-seal the ribbon ends. Using a dab of glue on the smooth disk at the front of the cufflink blank, secure the wooden disk in place centrally. Allow to dry fully.

Create a matching set
Repeat the process to make a second, matching cufflink to complete the set.

Cabochons cufflinks

🕐 Under 10 minutes per pair
£ From £3 per pair

Collect supplies
❏ A pair of flat-backed cabochons
❏ Cufflink blanks
❏ Strong glue

Secure the cabochons
Apply a dab of hot glue to the backs of the cabochons and press the flat surface of the cufflink

blanks centrally on to the back of each cabochon. Hold in place until secure and allow to dry fully.

Create a matching pair
Repeat the process to create a matching pair. If the cabochon has writing on it, or a motif that needs to be presented in a

certain way, ensure that both the cufflinks are positioned on the cufflink blanks with the cabochon in the same orientation.

▶ Cabochons cufflinks are the quickest and easiest to make – ideal for kitting out the whole bridal party. There are lots of colours and styles available from craft and jewellery suppliers. Select 1cm flat-backed designs to make them easy to secure to the cufflink blanks.

Button cufflinks

- ⏱ 30 minutes per pair
- £ Under £5 per pair

Collect supplies
- ❏ Four 1.5cm round shell buttons
- ❏ Two small heart motif shell buttons
- ❏ Two 10cm lengths of silver-plated 0.80mm wire
- ❏ Jewellery pliers

Create the upper section

With the small heart button layered on top of the round button, feed the wire through both holes on one side of the buttons and back down through the holes on the other side. Press the wire flat to the surface of the button with 3cm–4cm of wire passed through it. Use the jewellery pliers to neatly wrap the wire tail around the stem three or four times and trim.

Add the base button

Slide the wire through the hole in the round button, working from the back of the button to the front. Slide the button down until there's 1.5cm of wire between the two sets of buttons.

Secure the wire ends

Repeat the wrapping process to secure the second wire tail between the two buttons before trimming the ends.
Use the pliers to press the wraps to secure them tightly against the stem and to remove any sharp points.

Make the second cufflink

Repeat the process to make a second, matching cufflink. The cufflinks can be easily slipped though the holes in the shirt cuffs ready to wear.

Stitched monogram cufflinks

- ⏱ 40 minutes per pair
- £ Under £5 per pair

Collect supplies
- ❏ Two cover buttons
- ❏ Pair of silver cufflink blanks
- ❏ Linen fabric
- ❏ Embroidery threads
- ❏ Embroidery needle
- ❏ Air erasable pen
- ❏ Jewellery pliers
- ❏ Strong glue

Mark out the design

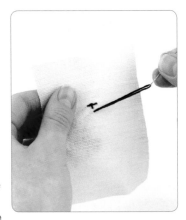

Using the template included in the cover button pack, mark out the fabric required to cover the button. Working inside these guide lines, draw out the monogram initials. Add a border if desired. Using a length of embroidery thread, stitch the design with neat even back stitches.

Stitch the design

Following the instructions for the cover button, secure the stitched monogram on to the centre of the button front and secure the back firmly to hold the stitched monogram in place.

Secure to the cufflink blank

Using jewellery pliers, snip away the button shank. Secure the button on to the front disk of the cufflink blank with a dab of strong glue. Repeat the process to create a second, matching cufflink.

Ties, bow ties and cravats

Make your own accessories in your chosen colour and style with this simple sewing guide.

Ties and bow ties can be made up in any colour to suit your theme. Pretty print fabrics are a great way to add in some fun to your wedding.

Standard tie

- 🕐 Up to 3 hours per tie
- £ Under £10 per tie

Collect supplies

- ❑ 1m silk fabric
- ❑ 1m medium weight lining cotton
- ❑ Rotary cutter and mat
- ❑ Needle and coordinating threads
- ❑ Sewing machine
- ❑ Pins
- ❑ Dressmaker's scissors
- ❑ Tie pattern (see tie pattern guide opposite)

Cut the pieces

Using the pattern pieces created, place along the bias (45° across the grain of the fabric) and pin in place. Cut out one of each from the silk, repeat to create one of each from the lining fabric.

Join into a strip

With the right sides facing, aligning the short diagonal lengths, join the three silk pieces together to create a long strip with triangles at either end. Repeat to create a matching piece from the three lining pieces.

Join the lining and the silk

Place the two long strips together with right sides facing and align the points of the triangles at each end. Pin together. With a straight machine

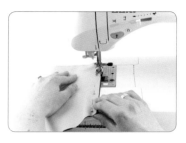

stitch, work with a 5mm seam allowance to join the two pieces together. Begin 5cm from the start of the large triangle, sew along the upper straight edge and round the smaller triangle, work 5cm down the second straight edge and fasten off. Leave the centre section of the second long edge unstitched.

Turn the tie through and hand stitch

Turn the tie through to the right side, carefully pushing out all the corners, and press neatly. Starting at the wide end

of the triangle, fold the outer edge to meet in the middle and pin in place. Continue working up the length of the tie, folding the unstitched edge under the stitched edge and pin in place. With neat hand slip stitches join the upper section securely to the lower section and fasten off.

Press the tie to finish

Remove all the pins and press the tie once more so it's neat and ready to wear. If you're working with a delicate fabric, place a pressing cloth, or a clean tea towel over the tie before pressing with the iron.

Make a tie pattern

Create your own tie pattern by following the instructions below and see illustrated guide in the templates section

Large pattern piece

Draw a trapezium that's 52cm long, with one end measuring 10cm and the opposite end measuring 22cm. From the centre of the end measuring 22cm, measure up 12cm and mark. From this marked point draw two lines to create a triangle on the end. At the opposite end, extend the upper line by a further 10cm. From the top of this line draw a straight line slanting back to the main shape. This forms an angled point – the slanting line will measure 14cm.

Centre pattern piece

Draw a trapezium that's 18cm long, with one end measuring 8.5cm and the opposite end measuring 7.5cm. At the wider end extend the lower line a further 11cm, draw a straight line slanting back to the main shape. This forms an angled point that measures 14cm. On the opposite end, extend the lower line by 10cm. From the top of this line draw a straight line that slants back to the main shape. This forms a second slanted point that measures 12cm.

Create the end piece

Draw a trapezium that's 33cm long, with one end measuring 7.5cm and the opposite end measuring 6cm. Working at the wider end, extend the upper line by a further 9.5cm. From the tip of this line draw a straight line slanting back to the main shape. This forms a slanted point that measures 12cm. At the narrow end, measure 5cm up from the centre point of the line and mark. From this point draw two lines slanting back to the main shape. This creates a triangle with the two edges towards the tip measuring 5.5cm.

Once used to cut your fabrics, the three pattern pieces will align together along the slanted ends to create one long tie piece.

Cravat

⏱ Under 1 hour
£ From £5

Collect supplies

❑ Silk fabric 32cm x 126cm long
❑ Dressmaker's scissors
❑ Pins
❑ Needle and coordinating thread
❑ Sewing machine

Trim the points

Align the two long edges and fold the fabric in half. At one of the short ends mark the centre point with a pin; trim the fabric to create a point, with each slant measuring 11cm to that point. Repeat at the other end to create a matching point. With the fabric folded right sides together, align the two long sides and the points at each end and pin in place.

Sew the cravat

With a straight machine stitch and using a 1cm seam allowance, join the cravat together along the three open sides, stopping the machine and pivoting on the needle to get neat points.

Begin at one pointed end, continue along the straight edge, leaving 10cm in the centre unstitched, and continue to sew to the second point.

Create pleats

Turn the cravat through to the right side through the gap in the unstitched seam and press. Fold inside the seam allowance on the gap and stitch in place with a straight machine stitch. Mark out the centre point of the cravat with a pin and make a series of even folds along the centre. Add pins at 3cm intervals at either side of the centre pin to hold in place.

Finished cravat

With a straight machine stitch, work a line of stitches along the centre point and at each 3cm interval to secure the pleats. Press the cravat carefully before wearing, ensuring that you don't work over the ripples created by the pleats.

Self-tie bow tie

🕐 60 minutes per tie
£ From £5 per tie

Collect supplies

- ❏ Silk fabric 45cm x 60cm
- ❏ Light-weight interfacing 20cm x 46cm
- ❏ Needle and coordinating thread
- ❏ Dressmaker's scissors
- ❏ Pins
- ❏ Sewing machine
- ❏ Template

Cut the tie pieces

Cut two tie pieces from the interfacing. Place the template on the bias of the main fabric (at a 45° angle across the grain of the fabric) and pin in place. Cut two shapes from the template, then flip the template and cut two more in the same manner. This will create four matching pieces, two for the front and two for the back of the tie.

Join the lengths

Lay out the pieces with the right side facing upwards and set out in two pairs, one for the front and one for the back – the angled edge on the thin ends will line up. Place the two pieces of interfacing on the wrong side of the back pieces and pin in place. Align the right sides of the two short angled ends and pin in place. Join together with a straight machine stitch. Repeat to join the two other pieces into two long lengths.

Press with caution

Be careful when pressing silk, as the plate of the iron can often leave a mark. Place a piece of cotton or a clean tea towel on top of the silk before pressing to avoid marking the fabric.

Sew the tie pieces together

Place the two long tie pieces right sides together, aligning all the curves and shaping, and pin carefully into place. With a straight machine stitch and taking a 1cm seam allowance, carefully join together. Begin stitching at the lower portion of one shaped end, work around the large flat end and across the long length at the centre before repeating the stitching around the other end, and fasten off. Leave the second long straight edge unstitched to turn the tie through.

Turn through and hand stitch

Clip the seam allowance on the curves and corners. Through the unstitched section in the tie, begin pulling the fabric through to the right side. You may need to use a pencil or a knitting needle to ease out the curves and the corners. Once the tie is through to the right side, press neatly and tuck under the seam allowance of the long straight edge of the opening and pin in place. Work with a neat hand slip stitch along the opening to join the final seam and press again to complete.

Press the tie

Press the tie neatly, using a pressing cloth or a clean tea towel if the fabric is delicate, to give a crisp finish ready to wear.

Fixed bow tie

⏱ 90 minutes per bow tie

💷 From £5 per bow tie

Collect supplies

- ❏ Two pieces of silk fabric, one 15cm x 31cm and one 8cm x 10cm
- ❏ A strip of silk 4cm x 50cm
- ❏ Needle and coordinating thread
- ❏ Pins
- ❏ Sewing machine
- ❏ Bow tie fastening set

Create a tube

With the right sides facing, align the two long edges of the larger rectangle of fabric and pin in place. With a straight machine stitch, work along to join together with a 1cm seam allowance. Turn through and press the seam to run flat along the centre back of the rectangle.

Create the bow loop

Fold the seamed strip over, aligning the two shorter ends with the centre seam outermost, and pin in position. With a 1cm seam allowance, join the two end sections. Trim the seam and turn the loop through so the seam sits on the inside of the loop.

Repeat to create a second smaller loop

Align the two long edges of the smaller rectangle of fabric, pin and sew together with a 1cm seam allowance. Turn through and press

the seam to the centre. With the seam outermost, align the two shorter ends and pin and stitch together with a 1cm seam allowance and turn through.

Insert the bow

With the seam of the loop positioned at the centre back, pinch the centre of the large bow loop and fold in the sides of the rectangle to create the shaping of the bow tie. Slide the folds through the smaller loop and position over the centre of the bow tie, ensuring the seam on the small loop is at the back. Work a few neat hand stitches to hold the centre loop and bow tie folds in place.

Create the neck strap

Fold the 50cm strip of fabric into a bias strip and press. With a straight machine stitch, sew along the length to join into a thin strap, concealing the raw ends. Feed one end of the strap though the buckle and secure the end with neat hand stitches.

Slide the hook on to the strap before passing back through the buckle to make the adjustable section. Tuck the raw edges of the other end under, and secure the hoop of the fastener into place on the short length of elastic with secure hand stitches.

Complete the bow tie

Feed the completed strap though the back of the centre section of the bow tie, moving along until centred. The strap length can be adjusted as required ready for wear.

Making bias tape

Cut a strip of fabric diagonally across the grain of the fabric. This is called the bias. This cut of fabric will have more stretch to it than fabrics cut on the grain.

The width of the strip can be made to your own preference, but it will need to be four times as wide as one face of the desired finished bias strip.

With the wrong side of the bias strip facing upwards, fold in half aligning the two long raw edges, and press to create a centre crease.

Open out the strip of bias and refold one of the long raw edges inwards to align with the centre crease and press. Repeat with the second long edge. Refold the entire length of the bias strip along the centre line and press firmly. The raw edges of the strip are now concealed on the inside of the bias tape.

Buttonholes

Present the men of the bridal party with beautiful handmade boutonnieres.

As with the ladies in the bridal party, male guests are offered a small floral decoration that's pinned neatly on to their jacket lapels. The designs given here show you how to make a range of buttonholes with fresh and fake flowers, as well as no-wilt fabric designs.

Thistle and pussy willow

- ⏱ Under 15 minutes per buttonhole
- £ From £3 per buttonhole

Collect supplies
- ❏ Sprig of thistles
- ❏ Three dyed pussy willow stems
- ❏ Natural twine
- ❏ Floristry tape
- ❏ Secateurs
- ❏ Buttonhole pin

Trim and layer blooms
Being careful of the spikes, strip away the excess foliage from the thistle and trim to 3cm from the base of the bloom. Cut two pieces of pussy willow to a suitable length, allowing one to be slightly higher than the thistle bloom.

Secure with floristry tape
Holding the blooms in the desired arrangement, secure together by wrapping with a length of floristry tape. Place the

buttonhole pin on to the back of the bloom and wrap with tape to secure. The pin should be facing outermost.

Add the twine detail
Wrap the length of twine around the wrapped stems of the buttonhole. Work up and down the centre of the stems before knotting at the front and passing to the back of the buttonhole to fasten off.

Twin tulip buttonhole

- ⏱ Under 15 minutes
- £ From £3 per buttonhole

Collect supplies
- ❏ Two tulips with leaves
- ❏ Floristry tape
- ❏ Secateurs
- ❏ Pearl-head pin

Trim the tulips
Remove the leaves from the tulips carefully, to avoid damaging them, and set aside for later. Trim the tulip stems with secateurs to 3cm.

Create a leaf
Holding the two tulips in the desired position, trim the upper section from one of the larger removed leaves. Position behind the tulips so that the leaf tip stands proud. Fold the lower sections of the leaf inwards to wrap around the stems.

Insert pearl-head pin
Use a length of floristry tape to secure the wrapped section of the stems and insert the pearl-head pin neatly at the back of the buttonhole ready to wear.

www.kerriemitchell.co.uk

Silk peonies

- ⏱ Under 10 minutes per buttonhole
- £ Under £3 per buttonhole

Collect supplies
- ❏ Two small silk peony blooms
- ❏ 2.5cm wide green grosgrain ribbon
- ❏ 1cm wide orange grosgrain ribbon
- ❏ Pearl-head pin
- ❏ Glue gun
- ❏ Secateurs

Trim the flowers
Using the secateurs, cut the stems of the silk flowers to 2.5cm and 3cm from the base of the bloom, to allow one head to stand slightly taller.

Wrap the stems
Holding the two blooms together in the desired arrangement, wrap the stems together using the green grosgrain ribbon. Apply dabs of glue to hold securely and allow to dry.

Complete the design
Place the orange ribbon around the centre of the wrapped stems for decoration and glue in place. Once the glue has fully dried, insert the pearl-head pin ready to wear.

Ribbon rosette buttonhole

- ⏱ Under 15 minutes per buttonhole
- £ Under £3 per buttonhole

Collect supplies
- ❏ 30cm of blue grosgrain ribbon
- ❏ 15cm of coordinating organza ribbon
- ❏ Decorative button
- ❏ Buttonhole pin
- ❏ Needle and thread

Create the rosette
Starting at one end of the ribbon, begin making small folds. Work stitches into each fold and draw up to secure. As you pull the thread the ribbon will start to shape into a rosette. Continue until you've created the circle of the rosette. Neatly secure at the back with a couple of hand stitches.

Create the ribbon tails
Trim the remaining rosette ribbon to make a 3cm tail. Cut the ends into a neat swallowtail. Trim the organza ribbon to 2.5cm and 2cm lengths with swallowtails, layer the ribbon tails together and stitch in place at the back.

Add the button and pin
Position the decorative button to the front of the corsage and the buttonhole pin to the back. Work the needle and thread through the corsage to secure them.

Speech writing

Use these professional tips for writing, preparing and presenting your speech.

James Hasler, professional toastmaster and master of ceremonies

Like it or not, the best man's speech is usually the make or break of a wedding reception. Not that I want to load the pressure on to your shoulders, far from it – here you'll discover exactly what it takes to make a great speech. Following these expert tips from James Hasler, a professional toastmaster and master of ceremonies who also runs HaslerHill Consulting, where he uses his expertise to enhance the performance and fine tune the skills of those already used to public speaking.

Forget the jokes

'Unless you're a comedian by trade, never try to tell a joke in your speech. Include funny stories – humorous anecdotes can be related to by any member of your audience, whereas jokes run the risk of falling flat. Jokes can alienate a large percentage of the group straight away and, as the delivery of the joke is crucial, if you're hit by nerves you won't be able to guarantee the results. Keep the context of your funny stories relevant to your audience – make sure that they're suitable. If the majority of the guests will be able to connect with the anecdote it will be good to share.'

Consider attention spans

'The audience you'll be speaking to at a wedding can be one of the most varied of any public speaking event – you might be faced with small children, your peers, and right through to elderly relatives. Try to aim for a maximum of ten minutes for your speech. The best way to check the timing is to read it out loud from start to finish, as though reading a book. This uninterrupted reading should last three to four minutes, which will equate to ten minutes of public speaking, with the natural pauses you'll make for breaths, punctuation and interaction with your audience.'

Preparation is the key

'Nothing can take the place of preparation before your speech, particularly if it's your public speaking debut. If you find that you're really battling with nerves, and you've enough time, it's great for the groom and the best man to attend a public speakers' club. These are local clubs run in most towns and cities around the country, allowing people to get up and brush up on their skills – even if you don't take to the stage yourself, you can learn a lot about delivery and pace simply by listening and observing others.'

Dedicate some time

'Giving yourself enough time also helps reduce nerves. Write your speech at least two months before the event so that you can rehearse it in front of the mirror – just like an actor, the preparation is crucial. When we watch professional stand-up comedians, it's all too easy to think they simply walk on stage and say the first thing that pops into their head, and their great humour simply floods through. In reality it's their professionalism that creates this relaxed appearance. They're so familiar with their material that nerves are diminished, and they're a joy to watch.'

Banish the nerves

'Lots of people worry about the number of people they'll be giving the speech to, which is only natural – it's often the largest audience they'll have had. However, what you have to say is more important than the number of people you're saying it to. If you know the subject that you're talking about the audience size will be irrelevant, as you'll be so much more prepared.

'The trick to feeling more relaxed with your audience is to connect with them. At a wedding there will be lots of people, many of whom you'll not have met before, and this'll heighten your nerves.

Quick guide to getting your speech down on paper

- ■ Write out the things you want to cover in your speech.
- ■ Put items into order and read the script in full.
- ■ Edit where necessary until you're happy with the content and order.
- ■ Read out loud to yourself; it should be three to four minutes of uninterrupted reading, which will equate to ten minutes of public speaking.
- ■ Practise the speech a few times until you're presenting it, as opposed to reading the script.
- ■ Use a timer to check the length of the speech, and edit where necessary.
- ■ Edit down the script into concise bullet points.
- ■ Practise the speech, checking the running time, until you're happy and confident in your delivery.

Calling in a toastmaster

The common perception of a toastmaster is a chap dressed up rather dapperly who shouts out names or directions at relevant intervals. This, however, isn't the case. One of the key traits of a professional toastmaster is that they'll ensure all your guests are in the right place at the right time and that everyone is enjoying themselves. As a professional toastmaster, James Hasler – who is a fellow of the Guild of International Toastmasters – recommends that when you're organising your wedding you should begin by seeking out one of the guilds or associations of professional toastmasters. The toastmasters affiliated with these guilds will have gone through rigorous training and assessment by their peers to ensure their standards are consistently high before they're accepted within those organisations.

Don't assume the role of a toastmaster is only required at the most formal and grand events. Many professional toastmasters, like James Hasler, have worked on a wide range of weddings, from every cultural background and across all budgets, styles and venues – so, with a little bit of research, and taking the time to talk through your wedding ideas with a few professional toastmasters, you'll be sure to find the right man for the job!

So prior to giving your speech, take time to introduce yourself to as many people as possible, try walking to each table, ask the fellow guests if they're enjoying their meal, tell them your name and have a little chat. They'll warm to you, and this will give you the feeling that you've some allies in the room – don't be surprised when they smile back at you when you deliver your speech!'

Create good prompts

'By practising your speech you'll find you don't need it written out in its entirety – a list of bullet points will be enough. Having your prompts typed out is a much easier way to read them than deciphering handwritten notes. If you've the facility at the venue to share images and photographs, this is a great way to keep your speech flowing, and your audience will enjoy it. The job of the best man is not to humiliate the groom, so choose pictures and related stories that are suitable for the audience – you can always use the more embarrassing ones on the stag night!'

Final words

'Avoid trying to boost your confidence with Dutch courage – my best advice is that you can drink as much alcohol as you want after you've delivered your speech. With the exception of the initial toasts, stick to water before your speech. The two speeches that stand out at most weddings are those from the bride's father and the best man, but these tips will help all members of the bridal party. Of course, you'll want your speech to be original and fresh on the day, but the groom can take

the precaution of finding out the themes or points of the main speeches, which will prevent any crossovers on the day or the same story being retold in two different speeches.'

Quick tips about toastmasters

❑ The cost of hiring a professional toastmaster can range from £250–£1,000. The pricing reflects the requirements for individual events. With mid-week and 'out of season' weddings becoming increasingly popular, you might find, as with other vendors, that prices are reflected in the bookings made at these times.

❑ When booking a toastmaster try to meet face to face, or at least have a few conversations over the phone, to find the toastmaster best able to accommodate the tone and style of your day.

❑ Many venues offer a wedding coordinator service, but this doesn't necessarily mean you won't require a toastmaster. The toastmaster will work alongside the venue staff and provide the polished finish that will ensure smooth running on the day. They also have the benefit of being independent to the venue and, should any problems arise, will ensure that your needs and those of your guests are put first.

❑ The toastmaster will be working to your planned schedule for the day. There are invariably lots of important features packed into a wedding, and he'll always be thinking ahead, keeping your guests informed and happy during the event.

❑ To an extent the toastmaster can act as a line of defence in disaster control. While he can't work miracles and prevent unfortunate incidents, he'll be able to act as a buffer, adapt and refine the schedule where needed, keep everyone informed of any last minute changes and take the stress away from the bridal party.

❑ Many toastmasters can accommodate all types of ceremonies, from the extremely formal through to casual and relaxed events. Chat through your ideas up front to find out the best toastmaster for your unique day.

❑ Booking a toastmaster through a guild provides a level of insurance. This will guarantee the level of service that'll be offered, and if unforeseeable circumstances prevent your toastmaster from attending another guild member should be able to step in without leaving you high and dry at the last minute.

Find out more

Discover the range of benefits of including a professional toastmaster in your celebrations by visiting James Hasler's website at www.toastmasterjameshasler.co.uk.

For more details about finding your local public speakers club and the Guilds of Professional Toastmasters, see the Useful addresses section on page 165.

ORDER OF SERVICE
Karen & Roger
13 March 2014
Belle Reve Motel

Welcome and introduction
Mrs A West, Registrar

Reading by Anne Styles
"How Do I Love Thee?"
by Elizabeth Barrett Browning

Declarations

Exchange of Vows

Exchange of Rings

Signing of the Register

"All You Need Is Love", The Beatles

Please join the newlyweds for
Champagne on the terrace

Chapter 6

The ceremony

From religious to civil, there's a wealth of choices open to you for your nuptials. In addition there's a considerable number of decisions to be made, and paperwork and planning to be handled. Here are some helpful guidelines to see you through the process, with a few creative touches to add to your special day.

Your wedding ceremony

The choice of ceremony is one that a couple will make based on their beliefs and feelings.

There are two main types of ceremony, religious and civil; and whilst the legally binding contract that's formed is the same the ceremony itself will differ greatly. A religious ceremony can run for up to an hour, with the vicar making the selection of the ceremony's content, while the couple will select the hymns and readings. A civil ceremony, which takes place in a licensed venue, can be much shorter, and aside from some essential legal statements the couple are free to select the other elements, provided they're non-religious in nature and content.

Legal requirements

Whether you're having a religious or a civil ceremony, there's a series of legal requirements that must be met before the marriage can go ahead:

❑ In order for the marriage to be recognised under UK law, it must be conducted by a person – or in the presence of a person – authorised to register marriages in the selected district.

❑ The marriage must be added to the register and be signed by both parties.

❑ Two witnesses also need to be present to sign the register when the marriage is added.

Changing your name

There's no legal requirement that a bride should take her husband's name after marriage, and it's becoming increasingly common for a woman to keep her surname and use the title Mrs to indicate her marital status. If you aren't changing your name, you don't need to notify anyone of this change of title. If you're planning on taking your husband's name your marriage certificate acts as proof of name change, and can be used to update the relevant parties – including your employer, bank, the DVLA, HM Revenue & Customs, council or utility bills and personal accounts. Aim to have all your details changed six to twelve months after your wedding.

www.kerriemitchell.co.uk

www.kerriemitchell.co.uk

Religious ceremony

For Church of England or Church of Wales ceremonies, there's usually no need to inform the Register Office, as the vicar will be authorised to register marriages. Before a Church of England ceremony, banns – notices of the proposed marriage – will be read in church for three Sundays before the ceremony.

Arrangements for Roman Catholic weddings held in a Catholic church will be made directly with the priest, ensuring you give three months' notice. You'll be informed of pre-marriage courses you must attend as a couple and will be requested to provide a series of documents including baptism and confirmation certificates, and a letter of freedom – a document indicating that you've not been previously married and are free to do so.

For Jewish and Quaker marriages the authorisation is automatic. For all other religions, if the officiant performing the ceremony isn't authorised then either a registrar must attend the ceremony or you'll need to have separate religious and civil ceremonies.

Other religious denominations, including Brethren, Baptists, Free Presbyterians, Methodists and Salvation Army, must obtain a certificate from the Registrar or gain a licence for a civil wedding, as their church officials aren't automatically authorised to issue certificates or licences.

Ceremonies for all other religions can take place, but you'll need to contact the Superintendent Registrar in advance in order to give notice of marriage. The Register Office will also be able to advise if the venue has been registered for marriage; if it hasn't you'll still be able to hold a religious ceremony there, but you'll need to have a separate civil ceremony in order for the marriage to be recognised by UK law.

Always begin by contacting your place of worship to find out the steps needed to arrange your marriage.

Civil ceremony

In order to have a civil ceremony you'll need to give notice of your marriage to the Register Office in your district. Most commonly the notice is given eight weeks before the intended marriage, and must be given a minimum of 15 days beforehand, and the marriage must take place within 12 months of giving notice. (The minimum 15-day period between the notice of marriage and the ceremony is to enable anyone with strong objections to protest.) You'll be required to supply a number of documents and other information when giving notice, including evidence of name, address and date of birth, details of any previous marriages and documents to prove they've ended (decree absolute or death certificate), and evidence of nationality – common documents to take are passport, driver's licence, birth certificate, utility bill or council tax statement. You'll be required to pay a fee to register the marriage, and there's an additional charge for the marriage certificate presented on the wedding day – additional copies can also be arranged.

Making compromises

You might be in a position where you have one set of beliefs and your partner has another. Just because you may therefore have different views on whether you should have a civil or a religious ceremony, this doesn't mean the marriage is destined for disaster! If you're married in a Register Office in England you can have a religious ceremony afterwards. You'll need to discuss this with both of your prospective venues and may be required to show your wedding certificate for the religious proceedings to take place.

www.kerriemitchell.co.uk

Licences and insurances

Alongside the ceremony itself, there are other legal considerations you'll need be aware of during wedding planning.

Once you've made the arrangements for your ceremony, you'll already have ensured that the venue is licensed for marriages. Here are some other aspects to consider:

Alcohol and music licences

Wedding reception venues offering wedding packages will be able to advise you of the alcohol and entertainment (music) licences that the premises holds. You're always able to request to see evidence of this if you're in doubt.

If you're having a DIY wedding reception and you find that the venue you want to use isn't licensed, it's often possible for you – or your caterer – to arrange a temporary event licence by submitting the details via the direct.gov website at www.gov.uk/alcohol-licensing.

Public liability

All of the wedding venues and staff working at a wedding should have public liability insurance. This protects and safeguards you against being sued for accidental injuries to third parties attending the event and their property. Most wedding services and suppliers will volunteer the information about the level of public liability cover they have when you enquire about making a booking, and of course you can always ask to see the relevant documentation for this.

Wedding insurance

Wedding insurance packages have different levels of cover at a range of price points. Essentially, the insurance will cover you should the wedding be cancelled due to something unavoidable. There'll also be coverage for damage to wedding clothes, and you can ensure that other elements are also included, from cakes and flowers, to gifts and rings. More comprehensive packages will include personal liability, legal expenses and personal accident. As with any insurance, however, if you decide to take out cover be sure to read the small print first. Check any exclusions and conditions before taking out a policy.

Same sex marriage

At the time of writing this book, The Marriage (Same Sex Couples) Bill, also known as the Gay Marriage Bill, was being debated in parliament, and the legislations on the issue received Royal Assent in July 2013.

This means that same sex couples will be able to get married in England and Wales now that the new measures have become law, and it is expected that the first gay and lesbian marriages will be take place in the summer of 2014.

The Act – which covers England and Wales - will allow same sex couples to marry in civil ceremonies. In addition, same sex couples will also be able to get married in religious ceremonies, where the religious organisation has 'opted in' to conduct such ceremonies and the minister of religion consents. This also aims to provide protection to those religious organisations who don't wish to hold same sex marriages from legal challenges. Further, this Act will enable same sex couples who've already had a civil partnership to covert this to a marriage if they desire.

Couples looking to convert a civil partnership to a marriage, or are seeking more information on Same Sex Marriages should check out the resources section on page 165 or visit www.gov.uk and search Same Sex Marriages.

Welcome sign

Make sure your wedding venue or reception is clearly visible to your guests with a pretty handmade sign.

Although you'll have included all the relevant information for your venue in the wedding invitation, adding a custom sign outside is a great way to ensure no one gets lost.

Paper doily bunting

- ⏱ Under 15 minutes per strip of seven flags
- 💲 From £2 per strip of seven flags

Collect supplies
- ❏ Coloured doilies
- ❏ Pencil
- ❏ Marker pens
- ❏ Coloured cord
- ❏ Paper glue

Prepare the pennants
Working on a single paper doily at a time, fold the upper section over by 2cm–3cm and press to create a crease. Repeat to fold all the doily pennants in this manner.

Add the lettering

Working in pencil first, draft out a letter on to each bunting pennant to spell out your chosen message. Work over each one with black ink, adding shading for a calligraphy effect if desired.

Affix the pennants
Position each doily along the length of cord, with the folded section passed over the cord. Use paper glue to secure the folded flap to the back of the doily to secure. Continue until all the doily pennants are secured.

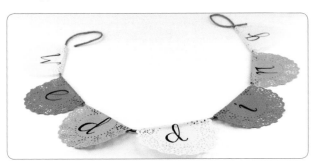

Chalkboard arrow

- ⏱ Under 1 hour, including drying time
- 💲 From £5 per sign

Collect supplies
- ❏ Wooden arrow sign
- ❏ Chalkboard paint
- ❏ Craft tool with drill tip
- ❏ Natural twine
- ❏ Silver pen
- ❏ Chalk

Create the hanging holes
Working carefully, protecting your eyes and fingers, mark out the placement for the two hanging-holes on the upper section of the arrow before drilling each one.

Paint the arrow and add a border

Working with short even bursts, cover the arrow sign with an even coat of chalkboard paint. Allow to dry, and reapply if required. Once fully dry use the silver marker pen to work around the outer edge of the sign to create a border of dots and dashes.

Complete the sign
Thread the natural twine through the hanging-holes, twisting together to create a loop before knotting to secure. Use the chalk to write your message on the front of the arrow.

Make the sign reversible
By painting and adding a border to the back of the arrow you can create a sign that can be flipped after the ceremony, either announcing 'Just Married' or even pointing out the direction of the reception.

Order of service

An order of service keeps everyone informed of the running order of your wedding.
Here are four designs to try.

Traditionally the order of service is used to inform the guests of the key members of the bridal party, include the running order of the service, and will feature the readings or hymns that are included. For more informal weddings, it offers guests a day schedule that similarly outlines the running of the event. Mix and match the ideas and craft techniques shown here to get the perfect order of service and schedules for your day.

Luggage tag order of service

🕐 Under 20 minutes per order of service
£ Under £3 per order of service

Collect supplies

- ❏ Natural card 7cm x 30cm
- ❏ Strip of lace-effect tape
- ❏ 20cm natural twine
- ❏ Luggage tag
- ❏ Alphabet stamps and ink
- ❏ Marker pens
- ❏ Pencil and eraser
- ❏ Hole punch
- ❏ Two small paper roses

Decorate the card front

Carefully stick the strip of lace effect tape across the bottom of the card 1.5cm from the bottom. Using the rubber stamp set add the words 'Order of Service' above the trimming.

Decorate the tag

Carefully write out your names on the tag in pencil before neatly marking over in black marker pen. Write the details of your day, or add a printed-out copy to the inside of the card.

Finish the card

Punch two holes 2cm from the outer edges at the top of the card and thread through the string. Push through the wired roses, twist the wire and trim off the excess. Loop over the decorated luggage tag before tying in a bow.

Icon day schedule

🕐 20–40 minutes per card
£ Under £2 per card

Collect supplies

- ❏ Card trimmed to 6.5cm x 21cm
- ❏ Blue card for backing 7.5cm x 22cm
- ❏ Selection of fine-tip coloured pens
- ❏ Pencil and eraser
- ❏ Template – if desired

Sketch out your design

Using the pencil, divide up your card into sections. Draw a scroll with your names at the top, then fill in the elements and times of each part of your day.

Ink over the design

Carefully work over the pencil outlines using a fine-tip black pen. Once the whole design has been outlined and the ink has dried, erase all the pencil lines. If you're photocopying the design, do so now.

Add colour accents and border

With a selection of coloured pens, work over the design to add a subtle touch of colour to each element. Place centrally on the backing card to create an even border and glue in place to finish.

▶ This picture-led schedule is great for more informal weddings. Unless you're a keen artist, keep the drawings simple – the ones here are included in the template section. Once you've sketched out the design and inked it over, photocopy it on to card to save drawing it out repeatedly.

Folded order of service

- 🕐 20 minutes per order of service
- £ From £3 per order of service

Collect supplies

- ❏ White A6 card
- ❏ Skeleton leaf paper red 10cm x 15cm
- ❏ Red handmade paper 9cm x 13.5cm
- ❏ Printed-out dates names and order of service title
- ❏ 30cm thin red ribbon
- ❏ Stick-on diamanté accents
- ❏ Inner leaves for order of service, printed, folded and trimmed
- ❏ Hole punch
- ❏ Marker pens
- ❏ Paper glue and strong glue

Create the front panel

Trim the skeleton leaf paper smaller than the front of the card blank by 5mm on each side. Trim the order of service title text and border with straight line, using a coordinating marker.

Decorate the front of the card

Affix the title text to the front of the handmade paper. Trim a neat 5mm border and glue on to the front of the card. Trim a length of ribbon slightly longer than the width of the card and glue 2cm from lower edge. Press some stick-on diamanté accents across the end of the ribbon.

Construct the booklet

Use the hole punch to create two holes 4cm apart along the spine of the card. Repeat to add corresponding holes to the inner sheets of the order of service. Place the leaves inside and thread the ribbon through the holes. Tie in a bow at the front.

Butterfly order of service card

- 🕐 Under 30 minutes per order of service
- £ From £3 per card

Collect supplies

- ❏ Printed-out order of service information in chosen font and colour on cream card
- ❏ Pink printed paper 15cm x 15cm
- ❏ Coordinated print papers
- ❏ Large and small butterfly punch
- ❏ Paper glue
- ❏ Scissors
- ❏ Stick-on gems
- ❏ Marker pens

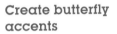

Trim and mount the card

Trim the printed order of service wording, adding a border with marker pen if desired. Mount on the front of the printed paper. Secure into position with paper glue.

Create butterfly accents

Using the large punch, cut a selection of butterflies from coordinating paper. Repeat to cut the same number of butterflies from the lighter paper. Place the smaller butterfly on top of the larger one and join with a spot of glue.

Complete the card

Position the butterflies around the front of the card. When you're happy with the arrangement, glue in place. Finish by affixing a stick-on gem to the centre front of each butterfly.

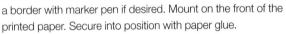

Order of service checklist

Here are some details that you might like to include in your order of service:

- ■ Names of the bride and groom
- ■ Names of the bridal party
- ■ Name of the officiant
- ■ Names of the witnesses
- ■ Chosen hymns, readings and music
- ■ A schedule of the timings of the event
- ■ A thank-you to the guests for attending

Readings and music

Add a personal touch to your ceremony with readings and music.

Having carefully selected readings and pieces of music makes your ceremony more memorable for guests, and adds a little extra to the day that you'll reminisce about for years to come.

Selecting readings

Modern and contemporary poems and song lyrics are becoming increasingly popular alongside traditional readings.

Officiants from both religious and non-religious services will be able to offer advice on the selection of the readings before you finalise them. This is, in part, to ensure they're suitable in terms of content (it's customary to keep religious readings for a religious ceremony only). If you're getting a little stuck with what to pick, they'll often have a list of suitable ideas to get you started.

www.kerriemitchell.co.uk

Whether you prefer traditional or modern, serious or humorous, think of your chosen reader. Aim for a reading that lasts no more than five minutes – longer extracts add a lot of pressure to the reader, and can break the flow of the ceremony. If you're concerned the piece you've selected is too long, consider breaking it up between two readers, alternating every couple of lines or verses as suits, or simply use an extract of your favourite section.

Adding a soundtrack

For many weddings the commencement of the ceremony is signified with the start of the music, traditionally the Bridal March, and music can be used again during the signing of the register, and finally as the couple leave the ceremony.

Consider the piece of music you select for walking down the aisle. As a bride you'll want to walk towards your husband-to-be at a lovely steady pace. Picking a song with a suitable beat makes this much easier than trying to walk slowly to an uptempo song. You could consider a more lively selection for signing the register or leaving the ceremony. As a basic rule, selecting three pieces of music will be sufficient to cover most ceremonies, although if you're keen to include more or less speak to your wedding venue and officiant to find out what options are open to you.

Depending on the venue of your wedding ceremony there will be a number of different music options available. A church might have access to an organ, for instance, in which case you'll need to arrange for an organist prior to the ceremony and discuss your selected music with them. Hotels, country clubs and other similar wedding venues often have a sound system installed, allowing you to play the selected music using CDs or MP3 players. If you're supplying music to be played on a sound system, ensure that you have a member of the bridal party or wedding venue staff on hand to play the set tracks. It's always worth having a little run-through before the day to make sure all goes smoothly.

Other venues might have the space to accommodate a live band or even a small orchestra, depending on your requirements. Any bands will need to be arranged and briefed in advance, and it's always wise to ensure that the venue has a suitable licence for whatever style of music you select – live or pre-recorded. If you're selecting a live band, be sure to discuss your plans with the officiant in advance, and ideally have a rehearsal with both the officiant and the band.

Ring pillow, pouches and box

Stow your rings safely with these four stylish hand-made designs.

Whoever you decide to present the rings during the ceremony, they'll no doubt be honoured. Creating a special pillow, box or pouch for the rings makes this aspect of the ceremony extra special, and it'll provide a fantastic photo opportunity.

Cotton ring pillow

- Under 30 minutes
- £ Under £5 per pillow

Collect supplies
- ❏ Two squares of print cotton 11cm x 11cm
- ❏ Thick wadding pad 10cm x 10cm
- ❏ 40cm of vintage-style trimming
- ❏ 25cm of narrow cream satin ribbon
- ❏ Needle and thread
- ❏ Pins
- ❏ Sewing machine – if desired

Join the two squares
Place the two squares of cotton with right sides together and pin in place. Working with a straight machine or hand stitch and allowing a 1cm seam allowance, sew around three sides of the square. Snip the corners of the seam allowance, being careful not to slice through the stitches.

Create the pillow
With the seam allowance trimmed, turn the pillow through to the right side via the opening, carefully pushing out the corners. Insert the stuffing pad and smooth out. Tuck the seam allowance of the unstitched edge inside, pin in place and slip stitch the opening closed.

Embellish with trimmings
Pin the vintage trim around the outer edge of the pillow, and with small neat hand stitches carefully secure into position. Mark the centre of the thin ribbon with a pin and position to the centre of the cushion on the front. Work a few hand stitches to secure the ribbon into place. Thread the ribbon through the rings and tie in a bow ready for the ceremony.

Decorated wooden ring box

🕐 Under 20 minutes

£ From £2 per box

Collect supplies

- ❑ Small wooden jewellery box
- ❑ Pencil and eraser
- ❑ Coloured marker pens
- ❑ Fine-tip marker

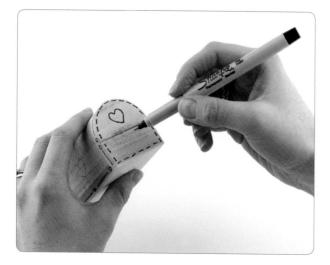

Add a border to the box

Begin sketching in pencil first. Draw a border of dots and dashes, or dots and lines, and add in chosen motifs.

Once you're happy with the design, work over the motifs in ink before erasing the pencil lines.

Personalise the box lid

Draft in pencil first. Add your names, wedding date and the words, 'From this day forth', or your chosen sentiment, on to the box. Alternatively you could add a line from a favourite poem or song. Once happy with the placement, work over the design in black ink and erase the lines.

Complete with coloured accents

Using a selection of coloured marker pens, work over the design adding in coloured accents to the motifs. Add the colour slowly to the different sections until you're happy with the design. Stow your rings safely inside ready for the wedding.

▶ Small wooden jewellery boxes are available in ready-to-decorate form from art and craft stores. Add your chosen motifs or design to customise it to suit your wedding theme.

Wedding rings

The tradition of the giving and receiving of wedding rings is believed to date back to the Roman times. Wedding rings are often a simple, solid band of precious metal – the continuous loop is symbolic of everlasting love. Historically women would always wear wedding rings, whereas men, influenced by the fashions of the time, may or may not wear a wedding band. Modern wedding bands can be as simple or as ornate as you wish – they can be worn by both partners, or only one. If only one of you is intending to wear a wedding band, be sure to advise the officiant in advance to ensure that this is taken into consideration during the ceremony.

Monogrammed organza ring pouch

- Under 30 minutes per pouch
- From £3 per pouch

Collect supplies
- ❏ Mid-sized organza bag 10cm x 12cm
- ❏ 25cm of vintage-style lace trim
- ❏ Six 1cm white buttons
- ❏ 3.5cm wooden heart button
- ❏ Pyrography tool
- ❏ Needle and thread
- ❏ Pins
- ❏ Pencil

Personalise the large button

In pencil, sketch out the initials of both of your first names on the heart button. With the pyrography tool, carefully work over to heat-etch the letters into the wood.

Secure the buttons to the lace trimming

Find the centre of the lace trimming and, using the needle and thread, with the buttons evenly spaced across the centre 8cm of trim, neatly hand stitch into place.

Secure the embellishments

Position the trimming band 1cm from the bottom of the pouch with the buttons centred on the front, and pin and stitch into place. Slide your hand inside the pouch to ensure that you

don't sew through both sides of the bag. Overlap the ends of trim at the back to neaten, and sew to secure. Stitch the wooden button to the right-hand side above the trimming to finish.

▶ Use a heat-resistant glove when working with a pyrography tool and follow the safety instructions provided.

Embroidered love letter ring pouch

- Under 1 hour per pouch
- From £3 per pouch

Collect supplies
- ❏ White felt 16cm x 16cm
- ❏ Pink felt 5cm x 8cm
- ❏ Selection of grey, blue and dark pink scraps of felt
- ❏ Pink and blue embroidery thread
- ❏ Embroidery needle
- ❏ Sharp scissors
- ❏ Pinking shears
- ❏ Embroidery pencil or air erasable marker

Create the envelope

Fold in the two sides of the white felt to meet at the middle. Fold the lower edge up to create an envelope. With the blue embroidery thread, work

along the fold with blue embroidery thread and running stitch to join together.

Embroider a love motif

Write the word 'Love' on to the 5cm x 8cm pink felt. Using the pink embroidery thread, work over the letters in back stitch.

Once the design has been stitched, place on the front of the felt envelope and stitch into place.

Create a 'stamp' motif

With pinking shears, trim a piece of grey felt to 3cm x 3.5cm and a piece of blue felt to 2cm x 2.5cm, and cut a small heart from the pink felt. Layer on top of each other before stitching in place on the top right-hand side of the envelope. Slip the rings inside ready for the ceremony.

Chapter 7

Photography

Capturing the special moments from your wedding day is a top priority for many couples, and can often be one of the larger expenses in your budget. Discover how to find the right photographer, and use these expert tips on getting the most from your photography package, posing like a pro, and getting the shots you always dreamed of.

Choosing a photographer

Capture your precious memories with wedding-day photography.

No matter how creative you are, you can't both be behind the camera and in front of the lens on your Big Day, so you'll need to seek assistance.

Wherever you live there will be numerous professional photographers who specialise in weddings and special occasions, each with unique styles and different packages for their services. Before deciding on the specific wedding photographer you'd like to use to capture your day, you'll need to take their prices into consideration at the early stage of dividing your budget. Every couple has different requirements regarding how they want to celebrate and remember their day. Some will want to allocate a proportion of their budget for a photographer, so that they'll have professional images to display in their homes; whilst others might prefer to use a larger part of their budget to fund a live band. The amount you decide to dedicate to photography – or any other element of your Big Day – is entirely up to you and your wedding day priorities.

The two most common options available to the soon-to-be bride and groom are hiring a professional photographer or assigning the task to a willing friend or family member.

So here are some helpful insights to help you through the decision making process.

Calling in a favour

Photography is an increasingly popular hobby, with more people taking up this creative pastime every year. Consequently you may be in the fortunate position where a friend or family member will offer to capture your wedding for you. Whether to accept this offer is a choice that only you'll be able to make – you'll need to decide how important the final images are to you personally. Remember, just because someone's a good friend, it doesn't necessarily make them a good photographer!

Of course, it might be that one of your nearest and dearest is actually a professional photographer, and offering their services for your nuptials is a fantastic and generous gift for you. But, to avoid disappointment it's important to know exactly what you'll be getting in advance.

www.kerriemitchell.co.uk

www.kerriemitchell.co.uk

www.kerriemitchell.co.uk

Photography checklist

Whether you're looking for a professional or an amateur photographer, here's a quick checklist to keep you on track:

Show your prospective photographer a selection of your favourite image styles

What some consider to be the epitome of romantic, others might find tacky, so let your photographer know what style of shot you like best. This might be tricky for a hobby photographer, who may not have the training or expertise to capture what you're hoping for.

Decide on the elements you'd like captured

Do you want a comprehensive collection of the entire day including the bride and groom getting ready, making your vows, exchanging rings, right through to cutting the cake, taking your first dance and enjoying the reception? Or, would you prefer simply to have a small number of shots to show the ceremony, and the family and guests in attendance? The more photographs you're hoping for, the more challenging this might be to a friend or guest who's stepping in to do the honours – it's rather a lot of pressure for them to be everywhere at once and enjoy your celebrations!

Alternatively, if you're only interested in a limited number of shots a professional photographer will often require you take a full-day booking, as it's unlikely they'll be able to schedule and accommodate another similar event on the same day. This may make the cost of the service seem relatively large in proportion to your requirements.

Receiving the images

Whether you use a pro or an amateur, you'll want to know how and when you'll be getting your pictures. Do you want the collection printed out and put into an album ready for you to look at? Or, would you rather have the images as digital files, ready to use at your leisure? Knowing upfront when the images will be ready could be an important factor in selecting your photographer.

Professional photography pricing and services

Seeing the cost of a wedding photography package can come as something of a shock. However, there's a lot more to it than simply snapping a button. Professional lifestyle and wedding photographer Kerrie Mitchell demystifies the process (and costs) of capturing your special day and gives an insight into understanding the price tags of wedding packages.

'Photography is expensive, but it's also the only lasting, tangible memory after your day is over. Your photographs are likely to adorn the walls of your home or have pride of place in an album or on your coffee table. It's so hard to "sell" photography because until the photos are taken a photographer can't show you how your wedding will look. It's also the only thing you pay for up-front and yet see nothing of until after the Big Day. The last thing you want is for the day to go by unrecorded, or even worse, be remembered only in blurry, out of focus or finger-over-the-lens snaps!'

What to expect

'A professional wedding photographer has many years' experience, has attended countless weddings, will be insured and will carry back-up equipment so that if anything should fail, they'll always be prepared.

'Most people have aspiring or amateur photographer friends with "nice" cameras. Ensure they know how to use them and, if you do decide to let them photograph your wedding, make sure they're prepared for the low-light conditions at the ceremony and reception. Relying on friends also means that they're under so much pressure to deliver that they probably won't relax much on the day.

'By hiring a professional you'll be guaranteed excellent quality photographs that capture all those little moments or details, as well as an artistic eye that someone without their experience won't necessarily have.

'Professionals also have access to professional-grade products, such as museum quality albums and professional photographic labs for the highest quality prints. Most professionals turn up at the wedding with lots of kit, like additional cameras and lenses, spare batteries and memory cards. They'll usually bring along specialist lighting equipment too, for shooting indoors in poorly lit areas.

'Meeting your photographer and telling them what you're expecting is always the best option. They can explain to you the exact difference between packages and help you decide on the option that's best for you.'

The final package

'After the Big Day, all the images from the wedding are downloaded and backed up on three different hard-drives, as well as a secure back-up online. A professional photographer then edits the images with special software, adding their own recipe of artistic touches along with any cropping or correction. Editing can take up to four weeks, especially at the height of the season, but it's this thorough attention to detail that makes it worthwhile to hire a professional.'

Kerrie Mitchell, wedding and lifestyle photographer

Find out more about Kerrie and view her unique photography portfolio at www.kerriemitchell.co.uk

www.kerriemitchell.co.uk

Writing a wedding photography list

Ensure you get photographed with all your nearest and dearest on the day.

It's traditional for the bride and groom to take part in a session of posed group shots. This is a great way to ensure that key members of the family and the bridal party aren't accidentally missed out of the photographs of this memorable moment.

Many professional photographers recommend that you write a list of your preferred group shots – which is wise, whether you're using a pro or a talented friend with a camera. This list ensures that no one who's important to you gets missed out, and is a great way to help keep people in the right place at the right time – otherwise folks do have a tendency to wander off to the bar or the toilets, or simply to enjoy your beautiful wedding venue, at the most inopportune moments! Once you've written out your list, be sure to pass a copy to a few key members of your bridal party and also the photographer; then they'll be able to help rally the right people into the right place at the right time. Give those selected to be included in these group shots advance notice that you'll want to have a photograph taken with them – it'll make them feel extra special and ensure they don't wander off when its time for their photo call.

Suggested group shots

Here's a selection of ideas for group shots. This basic guide can be adapted to suit your particular family circumstances or the size of your wedding party.

As a basic rule the bride and groom will be positioned at the centre of these shots and the other members of the bridal party will be positioned to their left and right, in relation to whether they're from the side of the bride or the groom.

- ☐ Mother and father of the bride
- ☐ Mother and father of the groom
- ☐ Both sets of parents
- ☐ Bride's siblings, groom's siblings
- ☐ Bride's grandparents/close relatives
- ☐ Groom's grandparents/close relatives
- ☐ Best man and chief bridesmaid
- ☐ Best man with groomsmen, chief bridesmaid with bridesmaids
- ☐ Pageboy and flower girl

Polaroids, videos and disposable cameras

Capture your special day with videos and guests' cameras.

Alongside the traditional still photography there are other options you may also wish to consider to document your day.

Video the event

There are numerous professional videographers offering services for weddings. As with still photography, professionals in this field come with a range of prices and packages. Much of the advice that applies to hiring a professional photographer is also true for videographers. Be sure to check you like their personal style, and that you understand, and are happy with, the delivery time of the finished package and format you'll receive. Alternatively, as the

quality of technology is advancing in leaps and bounds there are a number of great video recording devices on the market that can be used by a nominated guest or member of the bridal party.

Table-top cameras

It's common for couples to place small disposable cameras on the tables for the wedding meal or scattered around the reception venue.

Disposable cameras with a built-in flash function, often with a wedding-style housing, can be purchased from as little as £1.99, with the price usually dropping as the number ordered increases. Some places offer a personalisation service for adding wedding dates and names to the cardboard outer of the cameras. However, as this usually comes at an additional cost you may prefer to customise them yourself, using pretty embellishments to match your theme.

You'll need to have the pictures from these cameras developed, so unlike digital images this will involve an additional cost. There are a number of places both on the high street and online that offer services for developing disposable film cameras – if you're concerned about the cost, research the prices for this service up front, and set some money aside.

Set up a location for the spent cameras to be deposited by your guests so that they don't get misplaced. This could be as simple as a decorated box or even a large gift bag, labelled appropriately.

Quick tips for a novice videographer

- Use a tripod. This will eliminate wobbly shots that make the footage look amateur.
- Find a single spot for filming. In many cases, particularly during the ceremony, the wedding officiant or venue staff will nominate positions for the photographer and the videographer. Remain in these positions, as they'll provide a great vantage point without obstructing the event.
- Avoid trying fancy filming if you've no prior experience. Keep the shots steady and you'll have lots of material to be creative with while editing.
- Check the battery life. If you'll be filming the ceremony and into the evening, find an appropriate time to switch memory cards and batteries or recharge the power pack.

Laura's Bride Guide

With so many people using digital cameras or even smartphones, why not ask your guests to tag any images taken at your wedding with a pre-arranged hashtag? A hashtag is used to identify a search term online on many social media applications. If you're tech savvy, why not consider looking at the range of photo-sharing apps that are available for a range of different smartphones? There are some specifically designed for weddings, allowing you to create a profile for your wedding (usually online) and then invite your guests to join the event. By downloading the app and accessing your event or wedding profile via the app itself they'll be able to share the images they capture on the day. This is a great way for you to see your wedding through the eyes of your guests after the event. Search for 'wedding photo sharing apps' in your smartphone app store or search online.

DIY photo booth

Encourage guests to take fun snaps within a designated area at your reception.

A photo booth, a current trend in wedding guest photography, it's simply an area of the reception venue set up with a backdrop and a collection of fun props, the idea being that guests put on mini-costumes or accessories, pull funny faces or stand in silly poses, and have their images captured on film for the bride and

groom. Some professional photographers offer this service, usually at an additional cost. However, you can easily set up your own photo booth – but if you're hiring a professional for your other wedding photography it's a courtesy to let them know that you'll be doing so.

You will need...

❏ A dedicated area at the reception venue

Speak to the venue staff, as this needs to be in a safe place, not obscuring fire exits, the band or the DJ. Ideally, if this is created with a wall as a backdrop guests will be able to pose in similar positions in order to create the 'photo both' feel. Depending on the venue you might be able to use a closed window, or even decorate the wall, but this needs to be arranged with the venue in advance.

❏ A camera

A digital camera with a large, empty memory card is usually best. Some couples include a tripod, and even a remote control so that people can photograph themselves unaided – but remember, introducing lots of technology means some people won't feel comfortable using it!

❏ A selection of props

Get together a collection of different items, from hats and glasses, to feather boas and crowns. You might already have a few suitable items at home, or these can be easily found in party or charity shops.

❏ A frame to border the shots

Transform a large picture frame into a fun border by removing the glass and backing elements, then clean it and apply a coat of spray paint. Guests can hold this up to pose behind.

❏ A photo booth sign

Make a little sign to show your guests how to use the photo booth, and position it on the wall by the box of props.

Laura's Bride Guide

Many of your peers will be familiar with the photo booth idea, or will quickly catch on, but some of your older guests and relatives may not be so comfortable with it. Ask either the venue staff or member of the bridal party to keep an eye on the photo booth – they won't necessarily need to operate it throughout the reception, but it's great to have someone on hand to encourage guests to use it and to help anyone who wants to get involved!

Tips for posing

Even camera-shy couples can get wonderful wedding portraits.

Not all of us are naturals in front of the camera, but that's not to say we don't want a collection of wonderful pictures to look back on.

Alongside the collection of group shots you'll no doubt want a few shots of yourselves as husband and wife. Some couples find the thought of posing for these shots a real turn-off, and prefer a more candid style. If this is your desire, you'll need to let your photographer know so that they can capture such shots for you.

Whether you like the classic couple posed images, or a more reportage style for your couple shots, spend some time searching in magazines or online for ideas. Simply searching the terms 'wedding couple photographs' will offer a range of results and you'll be guaranteed to find ideas for your own pictures.

There are a few common poses each wedding photographer will like to include during your wedding day to ensure that you have a full selection of memories of the event. These often feature hands held together showing the rings, close ups of the couple's faces and full-length shots of the couple, with each photographer putting their own individual and creative twist on these pictures.

Portrait and close-up shots

Having a camera close to you can make you feel rather self-conscious, so if possible try to spend time with your photographer in advance, to help rid you of nerves. In order to capture your mood and happiness on the day you'll find that having a conversation prevents you from stiffening across your shoulders and having a tense, forced smile. Talking and making eye contact with each other and the camera will make it much easier to capture you looking relaxed, happy and beautiful.

The tone of the portrait or close-up shots can be changed simply by changing the position of your gaze – many traditional shots are taken with the subjects looking straight into the camera, but a more candid feel can be created by simply adjusting the position of your gaze – either to each other or into the distance.

Full-length shots

If you've already had a look at a few ideas for couples' poses in magazines or online, you can always try practising them together in front of the mirror, to help you feel less clumsy on the day. Of course, you don't want the poses to look staged or contrived, so come up with a list of up to five poses or variations for standing and sitting together to use on the day.

Your photographer will probably guide and direct you through a number of standing or sitting poses, but for a wider

range of shots consider mixing and matching between facing directly toward the camera, looking at each other or even looking away.

When looking at examples of wedding shots consider the elements that strike you most; the space or lack of it between the couple, the position of their arms, the direction of their gaze. Simply identifying the elements you both like will help you to communicate these to your photographer and achieve the shots that you want on the day.

Laura's Bride Guide

Most importantly, you'll both need to be yourselves in order to have pictures that you'll love to look at in years to come. As we had BMX bikes as the groom's mode of transport to the venue, we used these in some of the pictures, which not only made us feel relaxed, as they're familiar to us, but was also a lot of fun! However, if you're a more traditional couple, then trying to pose for a wacky shot that's really out of character might not work, no matter how much you love a specific example you've seen. So keep in mind that you both have unique personalities, and focus on showing those to the camera rather than trying to be someone else!

Chapter 8

The reception

Celebrating your wedding needn't be a high-priced affair. This chapter is dedicated to creating a wedding reception that both you and your guests will love, without the nasty hangover of a huge bill at the end!

Card box

Create your own postbox for your guests to drop off their warm wishes.

Amid all the excitement you won't have time to open and enjoy the assortment of cards and gifts you'll be given on your wedding day, so creating a designated spot for guests to leave these tokens will keep them safe until you've time to really appreciate them.

www.kerriemitchell.co.uk

▶ I customised a small vintage suitcase for the guests to put wedding cards in, with a little bunting sign. It looked lovely on the day, and we simply snapped the lid shut to transport everything safely home!

Wooden basket

ⓘ Under 20 minutes per basket
£ Under £10 per basket

Collect supplies

❑ Wooden basket
❑ Red grosgrain ribbon
❑ Heart-shaped doily
❑ Red handmade paper 9cm x 12cm
❑ Hot glue
❑ Two sets of fake cherries
❑ Fine-tip black marker
❑ Pencil and eraser
❑ Paper scissors

Secure the ribbon

Starting at the back of the basket, secure one end of the ribbon with hot glue. Begin wrapping around the centre of the basket applying glue at regular intervals to secure. At the front of the basket, slip the fake cherries over the ribbon, sandwiching one stalk to secure it to the basket. Continue securing the ribbon, adding the second set of cherries at the other side of the front of the basket. Neatly fix the ribbon at the back of the basket.

Create tag

Trim the red handmade paper to a heart shape that fits in the centre of the doily and glue in place to create a neat border. Write message 'Bride & Groom' or your names on the paper in pencil. Work over in marker pen and erase pencil lines when dry.

Secure the tag

Using small dabs of glue, secure the heart motif to the centre of the front panel of the basket over the ribbon. Place the basket in your reception venue ready for guests' cards.

▶ Wooden and woven baskets are available from craft and home decoration stores in a range of colours, shapes, sizes and styles. Hunt about to find the right size and design – not to mention price – for your wedding!

Wrapped-gift card box

🕑 Under 20 minutes per box
£ Under £3 per box

Collect supplies
- ❏ Rectangular cardboard box with lid
- ❏ Pencil
- ❏ Ruler
- ❏ Paper scissors
- ❏ Tissue paper or gift wrap
- ❏ Paper streamer
- ❏ Sticky tape

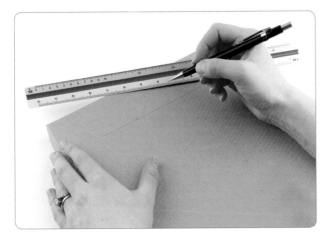

Mark out the letterbox
Using the pencil and ruler, mark out the section for the letterbox opening. Position on the upper section of the front of the box. Ensure that it's at least 3cm x 10cm – or larger if you have a larger box.

Cut out the letterbox
Using the scissors, neatly cut out the centre section of the box. If you're using a very stiff cardboard box try working with a craft blade and protective mat to neatly cut the opening.

Laura's Bride Guide

Setting aside a prominent little spot at your reception venue for your card box is a great idea. Guests will be able to find it easily and, if you have the space, they can drop off any gifts they've brought too.

Wrap the box lid

Place the box lid on to a piece of tissue paper or gift wrap. Working through the letterbox opening, slice the paper into four neat triangles from the centre point and fold them inwards to cover the edges of the letterbox. Tape in place. Fold the remaining paper around the lid to wrap neatly.

Wrap the box
Using the remaining tissue or gift wrap, neatly wrap the box. Using strips of paper streamer, create a cross first on the box lid, adding sections both above and below the letterbox opening and then on the main section of the box. Finish by adding a paper streamer bow before adding to your gift table.

▶ Depending on the number of guests, you can create a wrapped gift card box from any size of box, or make a series of different sizes, and place them together to appear like lovely wrapped presents.

Guest books

Creating a lasting token of the thoughts and words of your guests is a tradition many couples include in their celebrations.

Depending on the style of your wedding there are a number of different ways that you can capture the tender messages from your guests. Here are a few quick and easy ideas, whether you prefer a traditional journal-style book or something a little more creative.

Luggage tag book

- 15 minutes per book
- £ From £5 per book

Collect supplies
- ❏ Natural cover A5 sketchbook
- ❏ 2cm wide green grosgrain ribbon
- ❏ Three small wired paper flowers
- ❏ Two medium-sized silk-wired leaves
- ❏ Luggage tag
- ❏ Pencil and eraser
- ❏ Marker pens
- ❏ Strong glue
- ❏ Scissors

Create the tag
Drafting out in pencil first, write 'Guest Book' on to the centre of the luggage tag. Ink in using marker pen and erase the pencil lines. You could also include your names and the wedding date if you wish.

Add the motif
Position the ribbon along the centre of the book. Twist the wires of the flowers and leaves together into desired arrangement and wrap once around the ribbon.

Once happy with the placement, affix in place with strong glue, tucking the ribbon ends inside the cover to secure.

Finish with the tag
Trim the ends of the wire and position the tag on to the front of the ribbon. Glue in place and allow to dry.

Fingerprint picture

- Under 30 minutes per frame
- £ From £5 per frame

Collect supplies
- ❏ Mid-sized frame
- ❏ Linen paper
- ❏ Pencil and eraser
- ❏ Alphabet rubber stamps
- ❏ Ink
- ❏ Fine-tip black pen
- ❏ Pencil and eraser

Sketch the strings
With a pencil mark the centre of the paper for the position of the lettering. Use the pencil to work from this centre point to draw in the strings of the balloon. At the upper section, draw small figure eights to form the balloon knots. Leaving a gap for the lettering, draw in the lines for the ends of the strings. Using the fine-tip black pen, work over the pencil lines to neatly draw in the strings.

Add lettering
When the ink is dry, erase the pencil lines. Add your names using the alphabet rubber stamp, positioning the '&' in the space at the centre of the strings.

Position in frame
Omitting the glass, place the paper into the frame and secure. Present a selection of colourful rubber stamping inks for guests to leave their thumb or fingerprint – leaving a pack of wet wipes next to the frame will prevent your guests from staining their clothes!

▶ Leave a note to instruct your guests to add their thumb or fingerprint to the picture. After the wedding, slip the paper out, add the glass before reframing, hang on the wall and enjoy!

Best wishes pebbles

⏱ Under 15 minutes per jar
£ From £5 per jar

Collect supplies

- ❏ Large glass preserve jar
- ❏ Colourful doily
- ❏ Smooth round stones
- ❏ Length of ribbon 4cm longer than width of jar
- ❏ Piece of card
- ❏ Alphabet rubber stamps
- ❏ Ink
- ❏ Marker pens
- ❏ Colour-coordinated buttons
- ❏ Strong glue
- ❏ Craft knife
- ❏ Ruler

Create a ribbon slider

Cut an 8.5cm diameter circle from the card.
Using the ribbon as a guide, mark out two 1cm sections the width of the ribbon, 1.5cm from the edge at each side of the circle. Using a craft knife and ruler carefully cut along the two lines on each side to create slits.

Add your message

Using the alphabet rubber stamp and marker pens, mark out your message on the outer edge of the circle of card. Carefully weave the ribbon through the slits on either side and slide the card to the centre of the ribbon. Using strong glue secure a decorative button to each side of the card.

Complete the jar

Fill the jar with the pebbles, ready to be signed. Wrap the ribbon around the jar so that the card slider is positioned at the front of the jar. Overlap the ends and secure in place with strong glue. Separate the preserving jar lid and sandwich the doily inside before screwing on to the jar.

▶ Craft pebbles are available from arts and craft shops. Although this costs more than collecting them from the beach, they'll all be a uniform size and have smooth surfaces to write on.

Papier mâché guest book

⏱ 24 hours, including drying time
£ From £5 per book

Collect supplies

- ❏ PVA glue
- ❏ Water
- ❏ Papier mâché book blank
- ❏ Old unwanted book pages
- ❏ Paintbrush
- ❏ Stencil
- ❏ Black fine-tip pen

Apply the book paper

Tear the page of the book into small pieces. These can be as uniform or as irregular as you like.

Mix one part PVA glue with one part water. Working in sections of the book, apply a layer of glue, then with the brush apply a scrap of paper, dabbing more glue on to cover the surface.

Complete with a final layer of glue

Once the entire book has been covered, work over it with another layer of glue. Work in sections, allowing each to fully dry, until the whole book is covered.

Personalise the cover

Once the entire book is dry, use the stencil and black fine-tip pen to add your names and a message. Apply small sections of vintage lace or ribbons to the cover for a finishing touch. Leave small cards for your guests to sign and slip into the book for you to treasure.

Assorted inks

With a guest book you'll need to set out pens for guests to use. Add a message to a simple ceramic pot by simply writing on it in marker pen and baking in the oven at 170° for 30 minutes. Allow to fully cool before removing – the ink will be permanently fixed.

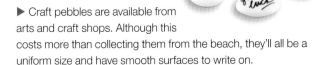

Favours

Traditional small trinkets are added to the place-setting for each guest – here are four quick-make designs.

Favours are a wedding tradition that dates back centuries. Originally they were sweets – a sign of luxury – but today couples can opt for anything, from small potted plants to their favourite confectionery.

Mini-seed packets

- 🕐 Under 15 minutes per packet
- £ Under £3 per packet

Collect supplies
- ❏ Vellum paper 5cm x 15cm
- ❏ Natural card, 5cm x 5cm
- ❏ Rubber stamp kit and ink
- ❏ Pencil and eraser
- ❏ Coloured marker pens
- ❏ Plant seeds
- ❏ Needle and thread or sewing machine
- ❏ Stapler

Make a vellum pouch

Score across the centre of the vellum paper and fold in half, aligning the short ends. Work a line of hand or machine stitches on each long side, 5mm from the edges, to form a pouch. Using pencil, mark out your initials and wedding date on the centre front of the pouch before inking in with marker pens.

Make the top tab
Score and fold the piece of natural card across the centre. Using the rubber stamp kit, add 'Love Grows' or a message of your choice to the centre of the front panel of the card.

Complete the favour
Fill the vellum pouch with flower seeds and fold the card tab over the top. Use a single staple to secure into place and seal the favour.

Heart-shaped sweet boxes

- 🕐 2 hours per box, including drying time
- £ From £3 per box

Collect supplies
- ❏ Papier mâché heart box with lid
- ❏ White spray paint
- ❏ Blue grosgrain ribbon 2.5cm wide x 60cm & 1.5cm wide x 24cm
- ❏ Strong glue
- ❏ Chosen confectionery or gifts

Spray the heart box

Covering your work area, separate the heart box and lid and give each a coat of white spray paint. Work in short bursts across the surface to give an even coverage. Apply a second coat if required.

Add a ribbon bow

Once the paint has dried, use the length of wide grosgrain ribbon to tie into a bow. Position on the centre of the lid and secure in place with strong glue.

Complete the box
Using strong glue, position the thin grosgrain ribbon around the outer side of the box, overlapping the ends at the back of the heart. Fill with your desired confectionery or gift and place the lid on. Allow the ends of the bow to hang down slightly, trimming them neatly.

Mini bottle of wishes

- 🕐 10 minutes per bottle
- £ From £2 per bottle

Collect supplies
- ❏ Small glass bottle, 4cm tall
- ❏ Strip of handmade paper
- ❏ Scrap of plain paper
- ❏ Glitter
- ❏ 10cm thin gold ribbon
- ❏ Strong glue
- ❏ Fine-tip marker pen

Create the label
Tear the strip of handmade paper to create a piece that's 1cm x 4cm – the torn edges will have a rough, natural look. Write 'Make a Wish' or you chosen message neatly on the paper using the fine-tip marker pen.

Fill with glitter
Using the scrap of paper, fold to make a small cone to fit into the top of the bottle. Remove the stopper and decant some glitter into the bottle. Add a tiny drop of glue into the  bottle, replace the bottle and shake well – this will adhere the glue to the inside and prevent it from dropping to the bottom.

Complete the bottle
Add a dab of glue to the cork before pushing into the bottle. Thread the piece of ribbon through the wire in the cork and knot to make a small hanging loop. Using strong glue, affix the written message on to the front of the bottle.

Embellished felt & organza pouch

- 🕐 15 minutes per pouch
- £ Under £3 per pouch

Collect supplies
- ❏ Organza pouch 7.5cm x 10cm
- ❏ Diamanté ribbon slider
- ❏ Needle and thread
- ❏ Felt 4cm x 4cm in two coordinating colours
- ❏ Small selection of pink crystal beads
- ❏ Scissors
- ❏ Chosen confectionery

Cut felt hearts
From the darker felt cut a heart motif that measures 3.5cm wide. Repeat to cut a smaller heart from the light pink felt. The smaller heart will be positioned on top of the larger one to create a pretty border.

Secure the hearts and embellish
Lay the light heart on top of the darker one and position on the corner of the organza pouch. Thread the needle and begin working around the  shape of the heart. With every stitch, slide on a crystal bead to sit on the surface of the heart. Fasten off securely.

Complete the favour
Fill the pouch with your chosen confectionery, pull up the drawstrings and position the ribbon slider in place before tying in a bow.

Top table decorations

All eyes will be on the top table during the wedding breakfast. Here are a few stylish decorations to impress your guests.

Adding a few trinkets to the top table will help to set the scene. If you're having speeches, it's customary for the speaker to either stand towards the top table or direct the speech towards you – with many of your guests reaching for their cameras, a few accents will really transform the table.

Paper heart garland

- 🕐 20 minutes per metre of garland
- 💷 Under £1 per metre of garland

Collect supplies
- ❏ Pages from unwanted books
- ❏ Printed floral papers
- ❏ Paper scissors
- ❏ Sewing machine or needle and thread

Cut the heart motifs
From the print papers and old book pages cut out a series of hearts – the more hearts you cut the longer or more garlands you'll be able to make.

Stitch together
Set out the hearts on a flat surface, alternating between the different print papers and old book page hearts. Using either a sewing machine or a needle and thread, begin joining the hearts together by stitching through the centre of each heart. Leave a long tail of thread at the start and end of the garland for tying up.

Complete the garland
Continue adding more hearts until you achieve your desired length, or make a series of different-length garlands ready to decorate the table.

Sewing on paper
Use a fresh, sharp needle and work with a straight stitch on a slow speed setting when sewing on paper. To be sure that the tension setting won't rip the paper, test your stitch on a scrap of paper before moving on to the final project.

Tissue paper pompoms

- 🕐 Under 15 minutes per pompom
- 💷 From £2 per pompom

Collect supplies
- ❏ Pack of tissue paper in a range of coordinating colours
- ❏ Thin wire
- ❏ Scissors
- ❏ Pencil
- ❏ Ribbon for hanging

Fold the tissue
Lay the entire pack of tissue paper flat, ensuring all the sheets are neatly aligned. Starting at one of the short ends, begin folding the pile of tissue paper back and forth until the whole thing is secured in a concertina fold.

Trim the tissue paper
Fold the strip in half and place the thin wire around the centre of the folded strip. Make a twist in the wire to secure it and trim away the excess. Using the scissors, slowly cut the folded end of tissue paper.

Finish the pompom
Carefully open out each layer of tissue paper, ensuring that you don't rip or crumple the thin paper too much. Once every layer of tissue has been opened out, gently shake each one to create the volume. Add a length of ribbon to the wire for hanging.

▶ You can make these with a single colour of paper. You'll need a minimum of ten sheets to achieve the lovely puffy volume.

Mr & Mrs 3D ornaments

🕐 Allow 1 hour per letter, including drying time
£ From £1 per letter

Collect supplies

- ❏ Papier mâché 3D letters
- ❏ Spray paint
- ❏ Chosen embellishments
- ❏ Strong glue
- ❏ Newspaper
- ❏ Strong glue

Paint the letters

Spread out the newspaper over your work surface, ensuring that you have lots of space around you – ideally doing this in the garden on a sunny day is best, as you'll have lots of space and essential ventilation. Carefully paint the letters. Hold the spray can 30cm away from the surface of the letter and work in smooth strokes, applying short bursts of paint.

Accent with trimmings

Wrap lengths of beaded wire around each letter. Use small pieces of tape or a dabs of strong glue to secure into position on the back of the letter.

Add ribbon details

Working with long lengths of 2cm wide ribbon in your chosen colour, begin wrapping around the shape of the letter. Secure the ribbon ends at the back with strong glue to finish.

Leave for your guests to decorate

Leave the white painted letters without embellishments and pass round during your wedding reception, asking your guests to sign them or add a little note to each one.

Chalkboard effect

Alternatively, spray each letter with chalkboard paint to create a striking finish. Decorate with chalks before the event – or ask your guests to decorate them on the day!

Hanging button heart

🕐 Under 2 hours per heart
£ From £5 per heart

Collect supplies

- ❏ Large collection of pearl buttons
- ❏ Silver-plated 0.80mm wire
- ❏ Fine 0.2mm wire
- ❏ Jewellery pliers
- ❏ Ribbon

Create the heart shape

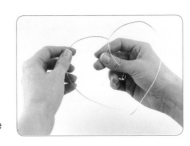

With the thicker silver-plated wire, fold a length of wire into a heart shape of your chosen size. Join the two ends together at the upper centre section with a twist – press with the pliers to secure any sharp edges.

Thread on the buttons

Lay out the buttons into a heart shape on a flat surface. Move the buttons until you're happy with the placement. String the buttons on to the wire, feeding it through two holes and leaving a small gap between each.

Secure the buttons

Beginning at the upper section, wrap the wire buttons around the heart shape, securing them together at the upper section. Wrap a length of ribbon around the upper section and knot to create a hanging loop.

Table centrepieces

Decorate the tables for added style. Here are four ideas to try.

The centrepieces you add to your tables can be as big or as small as you want. Larger designs are better suited to large round tables, whereas smaller pieces work best positioned at regular intervals on long rectangle tables.

Rustic-style cans

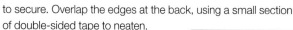

- ⏱ Under 10 minutes per can
- £ Under £2 per can

Collect supplies
- ❏ Tin can (washed and all sharp edges removed or taped)
- ❏ Wide-weave hessian 7cm x 25cm
- ❏ Green grosgrain ribbon 15mm wide x 50cm
- ❏ Double-sided tape
- ❏ Strong fabric glue

Secure the hessian
Wrap a length of double-sided tape around the centre of the can. Peel away the backing paper and press the hessian in place on the can to secure. Overlap the edges at the back, using a small section of double-sided tape to neaten.

Create a fixed bow
Trim the grosgrain ribbons into lengths of 24cm, 20cm and 6cm. Fold the two ends of the 20cm length of ribbon into the centre and secure in place with a dab of strong fabric glue. Place this loop in the centre of the 6cm strip with the join facing upwards. Fold the ends of the ribbon over and secure in place with a dab of fabric glue.

Add the accent
Work along the 24cm length of ribbon with fabric glue and wrap around the centre of the hessian strip to secure in place, overlapping and neatening the ends at the back. Once dry, position the fixed bow on the front with a generous dab of fabric glue.

▶ Hessian is tricky to cut neatly, so press with an iron before cutting with a rotary cutter and ruler. The edges will fray slightly, giving a lovely rustic feel!

Vintage glass votive candle holders

- ⏱ Under 5 minutes
- £ From £5 per pair

Collect supplies
- ❏ Vintage glasses
- ❏ Votive candles that fit easily inside the glasses
- ❏ Selection of ribbons in complementary finishes and widths
- ❏ Strong glue

Trim the ribbon ends
With sharp fabric scissors, trim the ends of the ribbons, some with swallowtails and others diagonally for contrast.

Layer the ribbons
Mark the centre point of both ribbons. Add a small dab of glue to the centre point of the thinner ribbon and work 5cm of glue to either side of it. Position on top of the wider ribbon so that it sits centrally, and press in place.

Secure layered bow
Add a dab of glue to the back of the glass and wrap the layered ribbon around the centre of the glass, knotting tightly at the front. Taking the wider ribbon first, tie in a neat bow. Bring the narrower ribbon to the front in between the loop and the tail of the previous bow on each side and knot tightly before tying a second bow to sit at the front.

▶ Vintage glasses come in a wide range of colours. Pick either complementary or contrasting ribbons in a range of finishes for different effects.

Vintage teacup candles

🕐 30 minutes' preparation, plus several hours wax-setting time
💷 From £5 per candle

Collect supplies
- ❏ Soy wax shavings
- ❏ Candle wick
- ❏ Can (to melt wax in)
- ❏ Saucepan
- ❏ Scented oil/wax (optional)
- ❏ Vintage teacup and saucer
- ❏ Plastic mixing spoon
- ❏ Small stick (cakepop or lolly stick))
- ❏ Adhesive tape

Melt the wax
Place the wick in the centre of the cup. Balance the small stick across the rim with the wick resting against it. Tape the wick to the stick to hold it in place centrally, with the metal plate flush on the bottom of the cup.

Fill the teacup
Pour twice the teacup's volume of wax shavings into the can and place in a saucepan of boiling water to create a bain-marie. Gently melt the wax until all the shavings disappear to leave a golden liquid with a honey consistency. If you're adding scented wax or oil, do so now and mix slowly. Take the can of wax off the heat and allow to cool until the surface begins to thicken, but not solidify. Slowly pour the melted wax into the teacup.

Leave to set
Once poured into the teacup, the wax may take several hours to fully set depending on the room temperature. Moving or touching the surface before it's fully set will leave marks. Ideally, put it aside overnight to fully set. Trim the wick and place on the saucer before adding to your table.

▶ To avoid the risk of them cracking, ensure the teacups are slightly warmer than room temperature. Pouring the melted wax slowly and steadily will prevent air bubbles forming. Remember, the wax and the can will be hot, so use a heat-resistant glove when handling.

Feather vase

🕐 Under 15 minutes per vase
💷 From £10 per vase

Collect supplies
- ❏ Glass vase
- ❏ Red heart-shaped glass nuggets
- ❏ Clear cube-shaped glass nuggets
- ❏ Lengths of ribbon
- ❏ Wired butterfly motifs
- ❏ Large feathers

Layer the glass nuggets
Begin by placing the clear glass nuggets in the bottom of the vase, until the base is covered. Add a layer of red heart-shaped nuggets on top. Repeat layering until the entire vase is filled. Cover the top of the vase with the red heart-shaped nuggets.

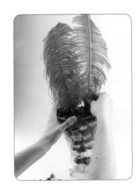

Insert the feathers
Push the large feathers into the glass nuggets and arrange so that you're happy with their placement. Insert the wired butterflies at the front of the design and arrange until you're happy with their placement too. The glass nuggets will hold the feathers and butterflies in place.

Add a bow
Take a length of ribbon and wrap around the centre of the vase. Wrapping it around a second time helps to hold it securely on the glass. Tie a bow at the front leaving trailing ends and trim neatly.

Selecting music

Music is a great way to add fun and breathe life into your reception.
Here are some popular options.

We all have wildly different tastes in music, and there are so many takes on what style of music to play at a wedding. Use these ideas to get you started on compiling a soundtrack for your special day.

A live band

The addition of a live band – whatever your musical preferences – is guaranteed to contribute something extra to your Big Day. Not only will they be supplying the music, but the musicians themselves also provide the entertainment. However, skilled musicians can be costly and often get booked up quickly. If you're keen to have a live band performing you'll need to take this into consideration early in your planning – ensuring that you have the funds to cover the cost and that your preferred band is available. As this can be a high-cost element in a wedding, be sure to check the venue is licensed for live music – some require additional coverage for live entertainment. Also ensure there's enough space for all the musicians and instruments – both for when they're performing and to prepare and stow their equipment. Check the stage or area for the band to be certain that there are enough power sockets, as it might be necessary to power amps, microphones and even a lighting rig – the band will tell you their requirements and suggestions for arranging the set-up.

Perhaps you have a group of friends that are keen musicians and would like to play at your wedding. This is a great way to keep the costs down, and many guests would feel honoured to be asked. However, it can put a lot of pressure on someone if you ask them to, say, play the cello for five hours straight, so consider a combination of pieces played by friends and family, coupled with a playlist of pre-recorded music.

Hire a DJ

There are numerous DJs up and down the country that specialise in wedding receptions – check with married friends and the wedding venue for recommendations. Again, you'll need to check with the DJ what space is required and also the resources needed, like power sockets and equipment storage. If you're avid music lovers you might want to work with the DJ to create a playlist of favourite songs and pieces of music – but do this in advance, to ensure all of your selections are available. Or simply let the DJ know a couple of your favourite bands, songs and artists and allow them to create a selection on your behalf.

Pre-recorded playlist

For smaller events, or if you're looking to keep the costs down, you can utilise your own music collection. Find out what sound system the venue has to determine the best format for your playlist – you don't want to spend a whole afternoon burning all your favourite songs on to CDs only to find you can play them directly from your MP3 player!

Song selection

Though it's important that the bride and groom have a selection of their favourite songs, it's always worthwhile adding in a mix of music that'll appeal to the wide age-range of your guests – especially if you want them to get up and dance, sing along and really enjoy the evening! If you're unsure what music your guests like, ask them to suggest a favourite song to add to your playlist on the RSVP cards.

Table planning

How to arrange a seating plan for your guests without the stress.

Planning the seating for your guests can be a bit tricky. However, the style of the catering and your selected venue often help you to see what's possible and what isn't – for example, your caterer and venue might be able to accommodate the guests on large round tables or a series of rectangular tables. Once you've confirmed the layout of the tables you can begin assigning the seats.

Seating on the top table

The top table is the one where the bride and groom sit, and is a focal point during the meal. Whether you have round guest tables or classic rectangular tables, they'll be arranged to complement the top table. Traditionally the groom sits to the right of the bride, with the places alternating between male and female guests – if the best man and chief bridesmaid have partners attending the wedding it's customary for them to be sat at alternative tables, commonly together. So, from left to right (facing the top table) the seating could run: chief bridesmaid, groom's father, bride's mother, groom, bride, bride's father, groom's mother, best man. However, how you decide to seat the top table is entirely up to you – you might prefer to only include the bridesmaids and groomsmen, and seat your parents together at another table. The 'sweetheart table', where the bride and groom are seated at a table by themselves, is a fairly modern idea that's becoming increasingly popular with couples. This is great way to relieve the difficulty of selecting the guests for your top table.

Getting the right mix

Some couples like to arrange the tables with people that don't know each other sitting together, in order to encourage mingling, although it isn't customary to split up couples to do this (unless one part of the couple is in the bridal party and therefore seated at the top table). Seating guests in family groups can discourage people from interacting with other guests; however, seating someone on a table where they don't know anyone can have the same effect. The aim is therefore to achieve just the right balance. Consider people's ages, interests, hobbies and pastimes when assigning them to tables.

Single guests can break the balance of the even numbers made by couples, and it's tempting to 'matchmake' by placing singletons together – but you should tread carefully, as this can make some people feel awkward; filling an entire table with single people can also make guests feel self-conscious. Ideally you should aim to mix your single guests with couples and families, to get the right balance on each table. It's customary to alternate male and female guests, with couples

placed opposite each other on long tables, or to mix them up around the table. The best rule to follow is to do whatever you think will make your guests feel most comfortable. If you're seating a table with small children, it might be tempting to place them next to each other, but try to ensure that they have one parent next to them – this makes it easier for the parent if they need to supervise or help the child with their meal.

Preparing your table plan

Start planning as early as you can. Once you've decided on the catering and style of the tables you'll know how many people you can assign to each one. Begin with your entire guest list, as this is the maximum number of people that you'll need to accommodate during the meal. As the RSVP cards start to come back you may need to remove some guests from the plans. Try printing out a list of the names and drawing the location of the tables; move the names around, testing out different combinations until you have just the right mix. Use a dab of Blu Tack on the back of each name to hold it in position – you may find in the final weeks running up to the wedding that the number of guests may fluctuate, and you'll have to rework the seating plan accordingly.

Keep it clear

Create a table plan that you can display in the venue, detailing the names of the guests and the tables they'll be sat on. This can be set out as a simple list, or with the names arranged in clusters to represent the locations of their tables. Adding place name cards on each table will help guests to find their seats quickly. Don't be surprised, however, if during the course of the meal some guests get up and switch seats – don't take offence at this, it's usually a sign that your guests are enjoying themselves and are mixing with others – in fact, it's a great compliment!

Table plans and numbers

Ensure guests are able to find their seats by following these ideas for stylish table plans and numbers.

The combination of table plans and assigned table numbers ensures guests are able to get to their designated seats without any confusion or mix-ups.

Framed table numbers

- ⏱ Under 30 minutes per frame
- £ From £3 per frame

Collect supplies
- ❏ Small frame
- ❏ Cream paper
- ❏ Pencil and eraser
- ❏ Fine and thick tip marker pens

Create a border
Working with the pencil, sketch a border of lines and love hearts around the paper, 5mm in from the edge. Once you're happy with the design, work over with the fine-tip marker pen.

Personalise the card
In pencil first, add your names and the wedding date to the top and bottom of the card. Add the phrase 'Eat, drink & be merry' around the outer edge of the card. Work over with the fine-tip marker pen.

Complete with a frame
In the centre of each sheet, write the table number or name. Use the thick-tip marker pen to ink in. Secure in a frame and add to the tables to finish.

Framed photo table plan

- ⏱ Under 30 minutes per frame
- £ Under £10 per frame

Collect supplies
- ❏ Print of your favourite photograph
- ❏ Frame
- ❏ Luggage tags, large and small
- ❏ Fine-tip marker pen
- ❏ Pencil and eraser
- ❏ Hot glue

Frame the picture
Trim your printed photograph to fit the frame and insert it securely, ensuring a neat, even border around the print.

Create the table cards
Taking the smaller luggage tags, write or stamp the name of each guest on a separate tag. Write a 'Take Your Seat' title on the larger tag.

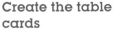

Position the tags
Using the hot glue, position the larger title tag at the top of the frame and arrange the name tags over the front of the picture until you're happy with the composition. Glue into place.

▶ For larger weddings, increase the size of the frame and the number of luggage tags, or make a series of different framed pictures for the different tables.

Wall-mounted card table plan

🕐 Under 1 hour
£ Under £5 per plan

Collect supplies

❏ Printed out copy of names arranged by tables in font and colour of choice
❏ Two sheets of dark blue A4 card
❏ One sheet light blue A4 card
❏ Small sheet of coordinated printed paper
❏ Ruler
❏ Pencil
❏ Glue
❏ Scissors

Trim the table names

Using a ruler to achieve straight lines, neatly cut out each table. allowing a 5mm border on each side.

Back the table cards

Place each table card in turn on to a sheet of dark blue card, trim to create a 5mm border on each side and glue in place. Repeat to back all the cards.

Secure the components in place

Trim 5mm from each edge of the light blue card and glue centrally on to the remaining sheet of dark blue card. Position the different table cards on the sheet

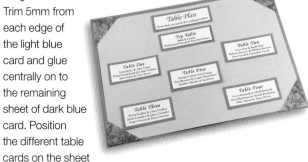

in desired position and glue in place. Finally snip the corners from the printed paper and glue into position on the corners of the table plan.

▶ Placing the cards on to the paper to represent the arrangement of the tables helps guests find their places quickly and easily!

Heart table number

🕐 Under 1 hour
£ Under £5 per number

Collect supplies

❏ Wooden heart motif
❏ Pink spray paint
❏ Lace trim
❏ Ribbon
❏ Strong glue
❏ Marker pen
❏ Letter stencil

Paint the heart

Using the spray paint, work in small even strokes

to cover the wooden heart motif, then leave to dry. Apply a second coat if needed. When fully dry, place the number stencil on top and sketch out the number in pencil, before working over in marker pen.

Add the trim accents

Working carefully with hot glue, affix the length of lace trim around the edge of the heart, leaving a small portion to overlap

at the front, and secure in place. Once the glue has dried, use small dabs of glue to secure the lace trimming to the front of the heart motif.

Complete the design

The wooden stem of the motif can be wrapped in ribbon or lace trim before being placed into a flower arrangement on the table or secured in a pretty vintage bottle.

▶ For a modern option, use chalkboard paint and chalk. For round tables, write the number or name on both sides of the motif – to make it easier to locate tables.

Place names

Pretty place cards for each guest are a perfect finishing touch.
Here are four styles to try.

Place names at the tables help guests locate their seats, and many people like to save them as a little keepsake from the day. These are most often simply folded, printed cards, which are great; however, with a little creative know-how you can stamp your signature wedding style on to each setting.

Speech bubble place card

🕐 Under 5 minutes per place name
£ Under 50p per place name

Collect supplies
- ❏ Dark card 6.5cm x 9.5cm
- ❏ Pencil
- ❏ Scissors
- ❏ Silver marker pen
- ❏ Template

Cut the shape
Using the speech bubble template provided, draw the shape on to the card and neatly cut out.

Write the name
With the silver marker pen, draw around the shape to create a frame. Neatly write in the guest's name in the centre. Write the names in a pencil first, to help to get the letters and placement just right.

Finish the place setting
Make two 0.5cm cuts upwards from the bottom section, spaced around 1.5cm apart. Gently fold the section of the card inside the cuts backwards, then slip on to the rim of a wine glass.

▶ Try alternating the direction of the speech bubble by flipping the template for a quirky touch.

▶ For a more romantic style, create a similar design using pink card and a large heart template. Or use any shape to match your theme – a butterfly, a balloon or even a cupcake!

Distressed luggage tags

🕐 Under 10 minutes per place name
£ Under £1 per place name

Collect supplies
- ❏ Two small luggage tags
- ❏ Alphabet rubber stamp kit
- ❏ Vintage brown distressing ink
- ❏ Scrap paper
- ❏ Thin ribbon
- ❏ Glue

Distress the tag
Remove the strings from both tags. Crumple up the scrap paper into a ball, press it on to the surface of the distressing ink, and then press on to one of the tags. The paper will leave a mottled inked effect on the tag. Repeat until it's covered as desired.

Edge the tag
Run the edges of the second tag along the surface of the distressing inkpad to add a little hint of colour. Using the alphabet rubber stamp, add the guest's name to this tag.

Construct the tag
Position the nametag on top of the distress tag at a slight angle, aligning the holes, and glue in place. Thread through the ribbon and knot.

▶ Selecting brighter coloured ink gives the tag a pretty marble effect – team it with colour-coordinated ribbon for a romantic style.

Vintage-style folded card

🕐 Under 20 minutes per card
💷 Under £3 per card

Collect supplies
- ❏ Lilac card 7.5cm x 10cm
- ❏ Coordinating print paper 6.5cm x 4cm
- ❏ Vintage-style lace trim 7cm
- ❏ Diamanté button or sequin
- ❏ Pencil
- ❏ Black fine-tip pen
- ❏ Paper glue
- ❏ Strong glue

Write the guest's name
Using the pencil, draw out guide lines and sketch the guest's name. Work over with the fine-tip black pen, adding shading to create calligraphy lettering if required. Once the ink is dry erase the pencil lines.

Create backing card
Mark the halfway point on the long side and score, then fold the card in half. Using the fold line as a guide, position the name on the front and glue in place.

Add accents
Position the strip of vintage-style lace trim over one corner of the place tag, ensuring that the name isn't obscured, and glue in place. Using a small dab of strong glue secure the diamanté button or sequin in the corner and glue in place.

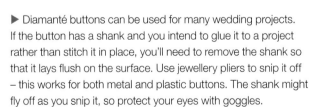

▶ Diamanté buttons can be used for many wedding projects. If the button has a shank and you intend to glue it to a project rather than stitch it in place, you'll need to remove the shank so that it lays flush on the surface. Use jewellery pliers to snip it off – this works for both metal and plastic buttons. The shank might fly off as you snip it, so protect your eyes with goggles.

Heat-etched dolly peg

🕐 Up to 20 minutes per peg
💷 Under £3 per peg

Collect supplies
- ❏ Dolly peg
- ❏ Pyrography tool
- ❏ Pencil
- ❏ Natural raffia
- ❏ Artificial leaves
- ❏ Strong glue

Mark out the name
With the pencil, neatly mark out the placement of the name. Whether you use script or block lettering is entirely up to you – you can even opt for a stencil for extra neatness.

Heat-etch the wood
With the pyrography tool heated to the correct temperature, carefully work over the pencil letters to add the name to the peg. Maintaining an even pressure and speed of movement with the tool will ensure neat results.

Add decorative accents
Position the artificial leaves at the side of the peg and wrap the wire stem around the upper section of the peg. Apply a dab of glue to the wire, and wrap a length of raffia around to conceal it. Tie in a small bow at the front.

▶ Pyrography is done with a specialist tool. If you've not tried pyrography before, get a few offcuts of wood to practise first. If you don't want to use this wood-burning technique simply write the names of your guests on to the pegs or use lettering stickers.

Safety first

All pyrography tools will come with a detailed manual with instructions on the best way to use the tool safely and to achieve the best results. Be sure to read this thoroughly before you begin, and work on a sturdy, clutter-free table, with the recommended safety equipment prepared before you begin.

Table games

These simple ideas will entertain guests during the wedding breakfast.

Having a few games set out on the tables is a great way to help guests break the ice. Similarly, small children might find the series of wedding speeches, or even the meal itself, rather a long drawn-out process, and providing something to entertain them will definitely go down a treat!

Mini quiz scratch-cards

- Under 50p per card
- £ Up to 5 minutes per card, plus drying time

Collect supplies
- ❑ Coloured card
- ❑ Quiz questions printed or written on paper, with the answers supplied below the question
- ❑ Paper glue
- ❑ Pencil
- ❑ Ruler
- ❑ Scissors
- ❑ Washing-up liquid
- ❑ Acrylic paint
- ❑ Sticky tape
- ❑ Glass jars

▶ Take your time to combine the 2:1 mix of paint and washing-up liquid. If you move the brush too vigorously the mixture will foam up!

Create the scratch-card coating
Mix together two parts of paint with one part of washing-up liquid slowly with a brush, to form a paste. Cut lengths of sticky tape 2cm longer than the width of the card. Attach them to the side of a jar so that only one end of the tape is secured, keeping the majority of the adhesive intact. Paint the non-adhesive surface of the tape with the silver paint mixture. When dry apply a neat second coat.

Trim the questions
Carefully cut out the question sheets and trim so that each one is the same size. Using the ruler and pencil, divide up the cardboard into sections that are 5mm larger than the questions on each side.

Create the quiz cards
Once the scratch coating has dried, trim the ends of the tape so that it's long enough to cover the lower portion of the card, obscuring the answer. Carefully press in place on the card to finish. Divide the cards into even bundles, tie a ribbon bow around each stack and place on each table.

▶ The scratch surface can be easily removed with a coin or a fingernail to reveal the answer on the card. The surface of the tape protects the paper underneath from being damaged.

▶ You'll need to apply two or three coats of scratch-off paint to fully conceal the words. And, test it on a scrap of paper first, just to be certain you're happy with the results!

Paper fortune-teller

🕐 Up to 15minutes per fortune-teller

£ Under £1 per fortune-teller

Collect supplies

❏ Print paper 16cm x 16cm
❏ Coloured markers
❏ Fine-tip black pen

Fold the paper

Fold the paper in half diagonally through the centre. Unfold and repeat to create a second fold through the centre in the same manner in the other direction. Using the creases as a guide, fold the corners of the paper in towards the centre.

Create the second set of folds

Turn the paper over and, working around the square, fold the corners into the centre point again. Once all the corners are pressed in, fold the fortune-teller in half through the centre, then open out and refold through the centre in the opposite direction.

Add the messages

Using the colour markers add coloured hearts to the outermost sections, then add numbers to the eight sections on the next layer, before finally writing the 'fortunes' on the eight innermost sections. Refold the paper and present on the table.

▶ What you add to your fortune-teller is entirely up to you – they can be wedding-related items, or can be linked to your theme, or can be sweet sentiments.

Children's colouring-in set

🕐 Under 10 minutes per set

£ Under £3 per set

Collect supplies

❏ Selection of plain white handmade papers A5
❏ Selection of coloured crayons
❏ Ribbon
❏ Small pail
❏ Fine-tip black pen
❏ Adhesive lace-effect trim

Create paper bundles

With the fine-tip black pen, write drawing suggestions on to the bottom of the handmade sheets ('Draw the wedding cake', 'Make a portrait of the bride' etc). Carefully roll the paper into a scroll and tie with a bow of ribbon. Repeat with a number of blank sheets.

Decorate the pail

Cut a strip of lace-effect edging tape, position it around the lower edge of the pail and carefully stick in place – alternatively use a strip of lace and some spray glue to secure it in position.

Add items to the pail

Place the scrolls of paper and a selection of crayons in the pail. If you're making one for each child, add a gift tag with their name on it and a ribbon to the handle.

Children's games

Some venues have regulations regarding the items given to children to entertain them – particularly if they're historic buildings and are keen to prevent accidental damage. Check with your chosen venue in advance of the Big Day.

Chapter 9

Food and drink

From Champagne to cake, and sit-down wedding breakfast to lavish buffet, deciding what to feed your guests is often a tough decision. This chapter will guide you through the minefield of catering and cakes, without a soggy vol-au-vent in sight!

Dining ideas

Stamp your personalities on to the traditional wedding breakfast.

Some venues – particularly hotels, country and golf clubs – have an in-house catering team, and in these instances you'll typically be selecting from a range of menu options, and may be able to sample the items in advance. If you've something particular in mind speak to the venue as early as you can to see if your requests are possible. Be warned, though, that while most venues will try to accommodate special requests, they'll also need to consider the number of guests, seasonality of foods and the time needed to prepare and cook, which may all have an impact on the overall cost.

Sit-down meal or buffet?

Aside from the specific food choices you'll be presented with, you can choose the style of dining. This is broken down into two main categories: a sit-down meal with the plated dishes being served in a similar way to the service at a restaurant; or buffet-style dining, where guests serve themselves from a range of foods at a special table. Sit-down meals are seen as the traditional option, though the food you offer can be anything but traditional, with couples opting for their favourite curry, bangers and mash, a hog roast or even fish and chips! Buffets can be a selection of hot and cold food and are a great way to accommodate a wide range of tastes and food preferences. Depending on the size and shape of the venue hosting your reception you might find that having a buffet is a bit awkward; if so an alternative would be to have a selection of buffet food presented on each table in a tea-party style.

Evening food

A second spread of food is often offered later in the evening. This is usually presented in time for the evening guests to arrive. Commonly, if a hot meal is served at lunch a cold buffet is offered as the evening meal, with a spread presented at a dedicated table from which the guests can help themselves. However, if you've opted for a buffet-style wedding breakfast you might want to consider offering something a little different for the evening meal; hearty warm dishes served in bowls that can be easily eaten with one hand are ideal for a late supper.

www.kerriemitchell.co.uk

www.kerriemitchell.co.uk

Whatever food options you choose to provide, it's a good idea to let guests know what food will be served and when. This is particularly handy for guests with children who'll need to keep on top of their little ones' eating routine.

What to serve?

It's impossible to find a menu that all your guests will love, so how do you accommodate their wide range of tastes? Sadly there's no simple answer to this! Modern couples simply pick their favourite food from a selection offered by the caterer, or request a specific dish or style of cuisine.

Dietary requirements can be tricky to accommodate, so it's prudent to enclose a reply card with the wedding invitations so that guests can advise you in advance if they're vegetarian or have any particular food allergies. Food allergies are serious, and in severe cases can be fatal, so you'll need to alert your caterer to such special requirements to ensure they're best equipped to serve your guests' needs.

Some venues and caterers are able to offer the choice of two different set courses,

commonly a meat or poultry dish and a vegetarian alternative. If you're giving your guests this option you'll need to know their preferences in advance, as the caterer will need to prepare the correct number of each dish.

www.kerriemitchell.co.uk

Sweet treats

Sugar-laden baked goods aren't only pretty to look at, they'll also go down a treat with guests.

Cupcakes, cakepops, macaroons and sugar cookies are a brilliant addition to the food offering at a wedding, whether you opt to serve them as dessert, use them to create an unusual wedding cake, or offer them around as part of the late evening feast. Here are a few tasty ideas for the bride-(or groom)-to-be who loves to bake.

Cinnamon and vanilla sugar cookies

Makes approximately 45 cookies

Recipe

- ❏ 450g (15oz) plain flour
- ❏ 250g (9oz) caster sugar
- ❏ 1 teaspoon baking powder
- ❏ 1 teaspoon vanilla extract
- ❏ 1 teaspoon cinnamon
- ❏ 1/2 teaspoon salt
- ❏ 240g (8.5oz) butter
- ❏ 1 egg
- ❏ Electric whisk
- ❏ Large bowl
- ❏ Rolling pin
- ❏ Non-stick baking tray
- ❏ Wire rack

Method

1 With the electric whisk, cream the butter and sugar together. Add the egg and the vanilla extract and mix until fluffy. In a separate bowl mix together the flour, cinnamon, salt and baking powder and add a spoonful at a time into the butter mixture whilst continuing to whisk. The mixture will be very dry and it can take some time to whisk it all together, but don't be tempted to add any more fluids to the mix – it's the dry consistency that'll make the cookies crisp and will help them to hold their shape better; if the dough is too wet then the cookies will spread when cooking and be gooey on the inside.

2 Once the dough has been fully mixed, place in the bowl in the fridge to chill for a couple of hours. If the butter in the dough is kept cold then the dough will remain stiff, making it better for rolling and cutting. If the butter content of the dough gets warm it will begin to melt and it'll be harder to roll and cut neatly.

3 Pre heat the oven to 180°C (160°C if using a fan-assisted oven). Roll out the cookie dough until it's an even 1cm thick. Using your desired cutter, cut the shapes from the dough, trying to use the dough's area as efficiently as possible. Place the cookies on a non-stick baking tray and cook for around 10 minutes. As these cookies have been made from a stiff dough they'll hold their shape, so when the edges of each begin to turn golden brown this is an indication that the cookies are ready. Remove from the oven and place the cookies on to a wire rack to cool ready for decorating.

Laura's Bride Guide

These cookies can be rather time-consuming to make. I suggest making the dough and cutting the cookies on one day and icing the next day. If you're planning on creating a base layer of icing and then adding a second layer of iced decoration it's best to add the second layer a day later, to ensure the base layer is fully set.

Icing a cookie

Collect supplies

- ❏ Fresh-baked cookies, cooled
- ❏ Icing bag
- ❏ 2 egg whites
- ❏ 500g (18oz) icing sugar
- ❏ 1 tablespoon of lemon juice
- ❏ Sieve
- ❏ Mixing bowl and spoon or electric whisk
- ❏ Food colourings
- ❏ Edible glitters and accents

Create the icing

In the mixing bowl, whisk the egg whites until they're fluffy and begin sieving in the icing sugar until the desired consistency is achieved – the icing needs to be able to hold it's shape, but not to be too stiff to pipe. Add the food colouring and mix until the colour is even. Mix for at least five minutes with an electric whisk before spooning into a piping bag. Store with the nozzle facing downwards and squeeze out any air bubbles.

Ice the cookie

Begin with a thin nozzle and work around the outline of the cookie to make a frame within which to fill with icing. Set aside and allow to set fully.

Freshness guide

Use this chart to check how long these baked goods can be stored in an airtight container:

Cookies	Up to one week.
Cupcakes	Un-iced two to three days, one day in the fridge when iced.
Cakepops	Up to one week.
Macaroons	Store in the fridge for up to three days.

Fill the cookies

Add a tablespoon of lemon juice to the remaining icing and mix fully to achieve a more runny consistency. Refill the icing bag and, working from one corner, and with even pressure on the icing bag, begin filling the outline until the surface of the cookie is fully covered. Set each cookie aside until the icing has fully set before placing in an airtight storage container.

▶ Adding edible sprinkles before the icing has fully set will hold them on to the surface. If you want to add any additional designs to your cookie with icing, it's best to leave the base layer of icing to set for a full day, where possible, before adding any additional details.

Classic vanilla cupcake

Makes approximately a dozen cupcakes.

Recipe
❏ 110g (4oz) self-raising flour
❏ 110g (4oz) caster sugar
❏ 110g (4oz) butter, at room temperature
❏ 1–2 tablespoons milk
❏ 2 eggs
❏ 1 teaspoon vanilla extract

Method

1 Cream the butter and sugar together in a bowl until fluffy. Mix in the eggs and vanilla extract a little at a time.

2 Add the flour a tablespoonful at a time and mix in. Add the milk gradually until the mixture is of a spoonable consistency.

3 Place the paper cases into a muffin tray and spoon in the mixture until the cases are half-full.

4 Pre heat the oven to 180°C (160°C for a fan-assisted oven) and bake for 10–15 minutes, or until the tops of the cupcakes are golden. Slide a knife into the centre of a cake: if the blade is clean when removed then they're done. Place on a wire rack to cool.

Icing a cupcake

Collect supplies
❏ Fresh-baked cupcakes, cooled
❏ 140g (5oz) butter, softened
❏ 280g (10oz) icing sugar
❏ 1–2 tablespoons milk
❏ Food colour in chosen shade
❏ Bowl and electric whisk
❏ Piping bag and nozzle

Make the buttercream icing
With an electric whisk beat the butter until it's soft, adding in the sugar little by little and mixing thoroughly until the icing is a smooth consistency. Once all the sugar has been combined, add the milk gradually, whisking until the icing is smooth.
Add a couple of drops of food colouring and mix until the colour is even. Begin with only a couple of drops – you can always add more to make the shade more intense.

Fill your icing bag
Add your selected nozzle and secure to the icing bag. Place the icing bag nozzle-down into a glass and spoon in the icing. When the bag is two-thirds full, squeeze out the air and create a twist to secure the opening.

Ice the cake
Holding the twist in one hand and the middle of the bag in the other, apply even pressure to push the icing from the bag.
Start at one side of the cake and begin working around the outer edge of the cake top to cover with icing. As you work around the cake, make the circles of icing smaller and smaller, to end in the centre and create a point.

Cakepops

▶ Using a cakepop pan will speed up the process and make uniform-sized balls, and you can use your favourite cake recipe.

Collect supplies

❑ Fresh-baked cakepops (cool on a wire rack and then place in the freezer for 1–2 hours before icing)

❑ Cakepop sticks

❑ White chocolate

❑ Edible cake decorations or sparkles

❑ Small plate or bowl

❑ Empty egg box

Melt the chocolate

Break up the chocolate and melt in a bowl over a saucepan of water as a bain-marie – keep the

water from touching the bottom of the bowl to prevent scalding the chocolate. Dip the cakepop sticks into the melted chocolate and insert one into each cake ball so it's about two-thirds of the way through. Put aside to set.

Coat the balls

Once fully set, holding on to the stick dip the cakepop into melted chocolate until fully coated. Allow the excess to drip off, then roll over the plate of edible sparkles to finish.

Finish the cakepops

Press holes into the top of the egg container to hold the cakepops until they set. Once set, store in an airtight container before making up in to desired arrangements.

▶ Ceramic pie beads make the perfect base for holding cakepops steady for display at your wedding.

Macaroons

Collect supplies

❑ 125g (4oz) ground almonds

❑ 200g (7oz) icing sugar

❑ 2 tablespoon caster sugar

❑ Half teaspoon cream of tartar

❑ 3 egg whites

❑ Chosen food colouring/flavour

❑ 250ml buttercream filling in chosen flavour

❑ Macaroon pan

❑ Icing bag

❑ Electric whisk

Create the macaroon

Mix together the ground almonds and icing sugar.
Using an electric whisk, beat the eggs until they form peaks. Add in cream of tartar and caster sugar and mix until fully combined. Increase the speed, add in the food colouring and whisk until the mixture is firm. Spoon the mixture into a piping bag and, using the markings on the macaroon tray, fill each one.

Cook the macaroons

Smooth out any raised sections with the back of a wet teaspoon. Leave to stand in a cool place for up to an hour before cooking for 10–15 minutes

in a 160°C (140°C if fan-assisted) pre-heated oven. After cooling for five minutes, carefully peel from the macaroon baking pan and place aside to cool fully.

Fill the macaroons

Mix up the filling, either whipping 250ml of buttercream – flavoured as required – or a spoonful of jam. Add a heaped teaspoon of filling on one

side and gently press a second half on top to create a sandwich. Store in an airtight container and chill.

Wedding cake alternatives

If you don't have a sweet tooth, wedding cakes made from cheese are a great alternative.

If you're looking for something really different, or are having a tea party and don't want to overload your guests with yet more sweet treats, a cake made entirely from cheese could be just what you're looking for.

Emerging from a trend that popped up a few years ago, the popularity of the cheese wedding cake has grown so much there are now a number of dedicated companies that create bespoke wedding cakes from cheeses. A great departure from the trusty old fruitcakes traditionally served up at weddings, an impressive-looking cheese cake will get your guests talking, and with so many wonderful British cheeses available you'll be able to combine flavours to ensure that there's something for everyone!

Professional offerings

There are many different options available for getting the perfect combination of flavours, design and even price. The cost of a cheese wedding cake is similar to that of a traditional fruitcake. However, if you're cutting the cake directly after the meal the cheese can serve as a final course, allowing you to reduce the number of different courses that are arranged with your caterer.

The fruitcake traditionally used for weddings can be stored for months after the day, and a cheese cake – depending on the types of cheese you select – has similar low-wastage potential.

Yorkshire Dales Cheese Company.

Yorkshire Dales Cheese Company.

Many cheeses can be stored safely in a fridge for several weeks, while hard varieties, like Cheddar, can be grated and frozen for use in cooking and sauces. Foil-wrapped Stilton, for example, can be frozen for up to three months, and when slowly defrosted will taste just as great as it did on your wedding day.

Creating a DIY cheese wedding cake

It's possible to make your very own wedding cake from a selection of fabulous cheeses. The experts at The British Cheese Board suggest following these handy tips:

Find a good supplier
You'll need to source a variety of different cheeses, using a selection similar to that found on a good cheese board: a hard cheese, a soft cheese and a blue cheese are often a good place to start. Select stackable wheels and vary colour, texture and flavour. Avoid fruit-flavoured cheeses, as these varieties are likely to leak fluid, which could spoil the arrangement.

Calculate the quantities
You'll need to allow around 100g of cheese per guest or a minimum of 10kg per 100 guests. Three to five layers, the largest at the bottom and smallest at the top, will create a traditional tiered-cake look.

Yorkshire Dales Cheese Company.

Presenting the cheeses

Place on a wedding cake stand or stack directly on top of one another with a circle of greaseproof paper between each cheese. Rustic bases are becoming increasingly popular – ask a local sawmill to cut and sand a slice from a tree for you, then wax the surface to seal it.

Finishing touches

Decorate with fresh or dried fruit, herbs and edible flowers, and serve with crusty bread or a tempting selection of savoury crackers on the side.

Fresh fruit

Fruit not only tastes delicious, but it makes a beautiful decoration. Try creating an elegant display with a selection of fresh fruits around your cake. This is a great idea to finish either a cheese wedding cake or a traditional fruit cake – your guests will love it!

Insider knowledge

Nigel White, secretary of the British Cheese Board, says 'Cheese wedding cakes offer a delicious, novel and cost-effective alternative to the traditional fruit or sponge cake. There are plenty of colour combinations and decoration options like fruit, flowers, feathers and ribbons, to fit your theme.'

His top tips for choosing the perfect alternative wedding cake are:

Nigel White, secretary of the British Cheese Board.

- Allow 100g of cheese per person; if you're offering the cake as part of the meal or buffet you can reduce the quantity.

- Choose the cheese on the basis of taste primarily. Using a selection of British cheeses is the best way to get a range of flavours.

- A cheese wedding cake should be a balanced cheese board, not just your personal favourites!

- Avoid particularly strong-smelling varieties, especially in summer. If a strong cheese is a must, check that the venue is sufficiently air-conditioned.

- Stick to decorating the cake with fruit or edible flowers – ivy is not a good idea, and bulbs, such as tulips, should have the stems wrapped before use.

- A good supplier will offer reliable advice and the opportunity to sample the cheeses you'll have on the day.

- Always try to look at the sizes of the cheese you want to use and make sure that some of those selected are evenly graduated wheels.

- Think about the colour combinations of the cheeses to ensure that the cheese wedding cake fits with theme of the rest of the day.

Find out more about the different categories of cheese available on the British Cheese Board website at www.britishcheese.com.

Wedding cakes and decorations

Create your dream wedding cake with these clever DIY ideas.

There are so many options when it comes to wedding cakes. You can order bespoke designs made to your requirements from a specialist baker, or enlist a friend or relative with a flare for baking. Many grocery stores offer iced but undecorated traditional fruitcakes that you can customise and embellish with decorations to suit your wedding theme.

Cake quantities

Use the chart below to help work out how many tiers – and what sizes – you'll need to cater for your guests.

Round cake		Square cake	
Size	Servings	Size	Servings
6in	12	6in	18
8in	24	8in	32
10in	38	10in	50
12in	56	12in	72
14in	78	14in	98
16in	100	16in	128

If you want a two-tier cake, but are concerned this won't be enough to feed your guests, get an additional tier of cake made up and set aside in the kitchen or serving area of the venue. This can be cut up and served along with the actual wedding cake to ensure no one misses out!

Love motif

- ⏱ 10 minutes, plus drying time
- £ Under £5 per motif

Collect supplies

- ❏ Wooden love motif
- ❏ White spray paint
- ❏ Two cake sticks (cakepop sticks)
- ❏ Selection of flat-backed glue-on crystals
- ❏ Strong glue
- ❏ Small strips of grosgrain ribbon

Paint the motif

Using the spray paint, coat the motif until it's completely white. Work in small sweeping strokes to achieve even coverage. Allow to dry fully, and apply a second coat if needed.

Add the gems

Working with very small dabs of strong glue, affix the gems to the front of the motif – you can place them in a line along the word, or scatter them at random if you prefer.

Secure the sticks

Once fully dry position the sticks on to the back of the motif and secure with a dab of strong glue.

For added grip, add more glue to the secured stick and position a small piece of grosgrain ribbon from the motif over the stick and on to the motif on the other side to bond in place.

▶ Insert into the upper layer of your cake, pressing the secured sticks deep into the cake to secure and conceal them.

▶ Wooden word motifs are available from art and craft suppliers and online – select any message you want, and embellish to suit your theme!

Cherry-topped cake

- Up to 20 minutes per cake
- £ Under £10 per cake

Collect supplies
- ❏ Pairs of fake cherries
- ❏ Thin scarlet ribbon
- ❏ Cocktail sticks
- ❏ Pre-iced cake in chosen shape and size

Create the arrangement

Working on the upper section, or the upper tier, begin arranging the cherries or clusters of cherries. Once you're happy with the positioning, insert one or two cocktail sticks close to the cherries to hold in position.

Add a ribbon

Cut a length of thin ribbon, wrap around the centre of the cake and tie in a bow at the front. If you have additional layers, tie bows around these too.

Complete the cake

For added drama, layer the decorated cake on to a second cake board; or you can add in more clusters of cherries for a stronger look or for larger cakes.

▶ Fake cherries are available from floristry suppliers and are a great way to add colour to a cake, rather than opting for fresh fruit, which can, on hot days, leak juice on to the cake and stain it. If you use fake fruits on the cake you could present fresh versions in bowls on the cake table.

Rose crown

- Up to 15 minutes
- £ Under £10 per cake

Collect supplies
- ❏ Pink 6cm wide velvet ribbon
- ❏ Pins
- ❏ Cakepop sticks
- ❏ Pink and white wired foam roses
- ❏ Pre-iced cake

Create a circle with roses

Bend the wire of a rose stem to create a circle – use two or three roses to create a larger shape if needed. Work around the circle, twisting the wire stems on to the circle to secure. Add the roses so that they sit above the circle of wire stems, creating a dome of flowers.

Secure to the cake

Once all the foam flowers have been secured into the circle, add the rose crown to the top of the cake. Position as desired and, moving the blooms aside, insert a couple of cakepop sticks through the woven circle and into the cake to hold it securely in place.

Finish with a ribbon

Pass a length of wide pink velvet ribbon around the centre of the cake. Fold the raw ends under at the back to neaten the join and secure in place with a pin. If you have additional tiers, add the ribbon accent to the remaining cakes too.

Cake stands

Save pennies by creating your own cakes stands. Here are some simple-to-make designs to try.

Cake stands remain the flavour of the moment and are often used at weddings. Whilst it can be costly to purchase a selection of different cake stands, you can create your own, at home, with a few simple supplies. These items were created using vintage crockery, so raid your cupboards and keep an eye open at jumble sales and flea markets.

Vintage glass cake stand

🕐 10 minutes per stand, plus drying time
£ From £5 per stand

Collect supplies
❏ Vintage glass bowl or plate
❏ Small vintage glass bowl
❏ Small decorative glass
❏ Hot glue

Affix the base plate

Position the base plate on a flat surface. Place the glass in the centre – mark the position if required. Using hot glue, draw around the base of the glass and press into position on the base plate. Hold firmly in position for a few minutes then set aside to dry fully.

Add the upper section

Once the base is glued firmly, work around the upper section of the glass liberally with hot glue. Lower the bottom of the upper bowl into place on the top of the glass. Hold firmly in place for a few moments, then set aside to dry.

Finishing touches

Once the glue has set you can turn the cake stand the right way up. Adding a ribbon bow to the stem of the glass adds a pretty feminine touch.
Or, alternatively, before glueing the bowl into

position you can fill the glass with seashells, ribbon bows, coloured glass or even confetti, to suit your theme.

▶ You can also adapt these to make larger, three-tier cake stands by simply adding another glass and large plate to the base.

Mismatched crockery stand

This single-tier stand was made by glueing an upturned sugar bowl on the base of a fancy plate, in the same manner as the vintage glass stand. You can even make a three-tier stand by using small teacups sandwiched between large dinner plates!

Decorated cake board

🕐 Under 15 minutes per board
💷 Under £5 per board

Collect supplies
- ❏ Cake board large enough to accommodate the cake
- ❏ Length of ribbon
- ❏ Length of lace
- ❏ Hot glue

Decorate the corners

Trim small strips of ribbon and lace to a length to fit diagonally across the corners of the base. Position the ribbon on first, over the edges of the corner, and glue in place. Layer the lace on top and glue to secure.

Secure the lace

Working around the edge of the cake base, secure the remaining lace to the foil surface with dabs of strong glue. Work carefully to cover the corner ends of ribbon and lace, ensuring that the glue doesn't mark the top of the cake base. Allow to dry fully.

Add a decorative bow

With a small piece of ribbon, tie a bow and trim into long neat tails. Position over one of the decorated corners and carefully glue into place to finish.

Three-tier vintage cake stand

🕐 Under 40 minutes
💷 From £5

Collect supplies
- ❏ Set of vintage plates – saucer, side plate, dinner plate
- ❏ Cake stand fittings
- ❏ Marker pen
- ❏ Screwdriver
- ❏ Drill
- ❏ Protective goggles

Mark the centre of the crockery

Using the marker pen, measure and mark the centre of the plates in turn. This will be a guide for you when drilling.
It's essential to be as accurate as possible – this determines the neatness and stability of the cake stand.

Drill the plates

Working on a non-slip surface that isn't going to be damaged by the drill, add a few drops of cold water to the surface of the crockery (to keep the drill bit from getting too hot!) and carefully drill holes into the centre of each item, working from the upper surface through to the back of the plate.

Assemble the cake stand

Wipe any water or residue from the plates and begin adding the different sections of the cake fittings in place, using a screwdriver to tighten them as you work.

▶ Cake stand fittings can be bought from craft stores or can be found by searching online. They come complete with washers, so they're ready to use. Select a drill bit only slightly bigger than the screw sections of the fittings for a snug and sturdy fit.

Bar and drinks

Keep your guests' glasses topped up throughout the celebrations using these DIY savvy ideas.

Depending on the type of reception venue selected there will be several different options for the bar and the serving of drinks at your wedding. Here are a few ideas that will help you create the perfect refreshment selection for your day.

Venue with a bar

If your wedding reception is being held in a venue with a bar, like a hotel or golf course, there's often the option of placing a sum of money behind the bar to cover the cost of drinks, or else to pay a bar tab later. Most venues recommend you cover only beers, wine and soft drinks, and that those guests who require spirits and mixers cover the cost themselves. This not only helps to keep the bar costs reasonable, but also helps to prevent people from overindulging. Alternatively, the bar can be a pay bar, where guests purchase their own drinks just as at a public bar. However, if guests are to pay for their own drinks ensure they're aware of this prior to the event so that they'll know to bring some money along, as many of us don't carry cash these days.

Hiring a bar

If the venue doesn't have a bar and you're using an outside caterer they'll often have a bar service. With a mobile bar, depending on the size and space of the venue, you'll be able to select the drinks that are offered. Be sure to include a range of fruit juices and soft drinks for both children and those that aren't drinking alcohol. If the venue doesn't have a bar and you're looking to get a mobile service from a catering company, you'll need to ensure there's a licence for the event. Most caterers will be familiar with the process of applying for an event licence and will be able to make the necessary arrangements for this with the local council on your behalf.

Supplying your own

Alternatively, you can purchase a selection of beers and wines in advance and offer these to your guests with no charge. Buying bulk in advance can offer considerable savings on the bar tab. You'll need to decide if these are offered as 'serve yourself' or whether you'll arrange with the caterer to offer a bar, which may incur staffing charges. If you're offering the drinks free you may not require an additional events licence.

Reception drinks

Welcome your guests with a fabulous and tasty reception drink!

It's customary to offer your guests a drink upon arrival at the reception, and if the ceremony and reception are in the same venue the sharing of drinks acts as a perfect interlude between the two elements of the day. Many couples opt to serve a delicious bubbly to their guests, or even a mixed drink, like Bucks Fizz or Pimms, but here are some refreshing alternatives. Multiply these easy-make single serving recipes by the guest numbers, allowing 2.5 to 3 servings per person to ensure you have enough.

Elderflower Mojito

- 🕒 5 minutes
- 💷 £1.28

- ❑ 35ml Cuban rum
- ❑ 6–8 mint leaves
- ❑ 2 lime wedges
- ❑ 1 teaspoon sugar
- ❑ 75ml Belvoir Fruit Farms Elderflower Pressé

Squeeze the limes into a high-ball glass and add mint leaves and sugar. Churn, add rum and fill with crushed ice. Churn again, add more crushed ice and top with Elderflower Pressé.
▶ Ideal for a spring wedding

Summer Breeze

- 🕒 Under 10 minutes
- 💷 £1.04

- ❑ 10 or 12 ice cubes
- ❑ 50ml Belvoir Fruit Farms Cranberry Cordial
- ❑ 50ml vodka
- ❑ 4 tablespoons grapefruit juice (optional)
- ❑ Sparkling spring water

Crush the ice in a food processor and half-fill a tumbler or highball glass. Pour in the Belvoir Organic Cranberry Cordial, the vodka and a splash of grapefruit juice to taste. Top up with the sparkling water. Stir gently.
▶ Fruity summer wedding refreshment

Ginger Toffee Apple

- 🕒 5 minutes
- 💷 £1.20

- ❑ 15ml apple schnapps
- ❑ 30ml vanilla vodka
- ❑ 125ml Belvoir Fruit Farms Ginger Pressé
- ❑ 1 lemon wedge (squeezed)

Squeeze the lemon wedge into a tall sling glass. Add the apple schnapps and vanilla vodka before topping with the Belvoir Fruit Farms Ginger Pressé. Garnish the glass with an apple fan.
▶ Delicious autumn wedding treat

Mulled Sloe Gin

- 🕒 Under 10 minutes
- 💷 £1.42

- ❑ 25ml Belvoir Fruit Farms Apple, Plum & Cinnamon Cordial
- ❑ Boiling water
- ❑ 25ml Sipsmith Sloe Gin
- ❑ A splash of cloudy apple juice (optional)

Pour 25ml Belvoir Apple, Plum & Cinnamon Cordial into a mug. Add boiling water and top with 25ml Sipsmith Sloe Gin (and the cloudy apple juice if you're using it). Garnish with a slice of apple.
▶ Perfect tipple for a winter wedding

Alcohol-free options

Add a selection of tempting flavoured juices as alcohol-free options. It's wise to pick drinks of very different colours – for example, if the cocktail is a deep berry purple then select something in a zesty citrus for the alcohol-free variation. That'll prevent guests getting mixed up!
See more ideas at www.belvoirfruitfarms.co.uk

Table menus

Let your guests know the food they'll be enjoying with a handmade table menu.

Adding themed menus to each of the tables at the reception will inform guests of the upcoming meal. It's also a great way to let them know the order of the day's events, as you can include the timings for the speeches and cake cutting.

Contemporary card menu

🕐 Under 15 minutes per menu
£ Under £3 per menu

Collect supplies
- ❑ Wedding meal menu printed out on cream card in chosen font and colour
- ❑ Pink backing card
- ❑ Pink organza ribbon
- ❑ Scissors
- ❑ Ruler
- ❑ Glue

Trim the menu
Using the ruler, mark out a 5mm border around the edge of the menu text. Carefully cut around the card.

Add backing card
Place the menu on top of the backing card and mark out a 5mm border on each side of the menu. Neatly trim the backing card.

Finish the menu
Position the menu on top of the card and glue into place with an even border on each side. Once secure, pass the ribbon around the front of the card and secure into a bow at the top, allowing the ribbon ends to hang down. Trim to neaten.

Tea party menu

🕐 Under 45 minutes per menu
£ Under £2 per menu

Collect supplies
- ❑ Lilac cardboard 11cm x15cm
- ❑ Purple doily
- ❑ Pencil and eraser
- ❑ Marker pens
- ❑ Paper glue
- ❑ Template

Draw out the teacup
Use the template to sketch the teacup on to lilac card. Outline in black marker pen and carefully trim to suit.

Add the wording
Starting in pencil first, work over the design to add the details and also the wording for your wedding meal menu, adding your names or wedding date for a personal finish.

Complete with accents
Work around the design adding accent colours as you wish to the teacup motif. Place the teacup motif on to the centre of the doily and glue to secure.

▶ To save time, draw the outline then add the wording and neatly ink in before photocopying onto coloured card or paper. Then simply add accent colours, cut out and affix to a doily.

Tiered card menu

- ⏱ Under 30 minutes per card
- £ Under £1.50 per menu

Collect supplies
- ❑ Card
- ❑ Pencil and eraser
- ❑ Ruler
- ❑ Scissors
- ❑ 8cm of thin ribbon
- ❑ Hole punch
- ❑ Fine-tip markers

Cut and score card
Trim the card into five 5cm wide pieces measuring 5cm, 6.5cm, 8cm, 9.5cm and 11.5cm. Using the ruler, carefully score each piece of card 1.5cm down from the top edge.

Write out your menu

Using the pencil to draft out the words, write the different courses of the wedding menu on each section, so that when layered only the course names are visible. Write your names and dates on the lower section of card before inking in.

Construct the layers

Align the scored upper section and punch two holes 1cm from each outer edge. Feed the ribbon through and tie in a bow at the front.

▶ If you're having more courses, simply add another piece of card 1.5cm longer than the one for the previous course.

Gatefold ribbon slider menu

- ⏱ Under 20 minutes per menu
- £ Under £2 per menu

Collect supplies
- ❑ Gatefold A6 card
- ❑ Printed paper
- ❑ Wedding menu printed on card in chosen font and colour
- ❑ Coloured marker pens
- ❑ Glue
- ❑ Blue 2cm wide grosgrain ribbon
- ❑ Paper glue
- ❑ Strong glue
- ❑ Scissors
- ❑ Template

Insert the menu
Trim the print paper to the same size as the inside of the card blank, and the menu to the required size. Use the marker pens to add a double border to the print paper and a single border to the printed menu. Position the menu centrally on the print paper before glueing both inside the card.

Create the front motif

Use the template to create the scalloped motif for the front of the card. Carefully cut out and add a double border using marker pens before writing 'Menu' in the centre. Use the strong glue to affix to the centre of the ribbon.

Finish with a ribbon slider

Close the card and place the ribbon around the card holding the gatefolds shut. On the reverse add

a dab of strong glue to secure the ribbon ends together. The ribbon should not be glued to the card and should be tight enough to hold the card closed but easy to slip off.

Chapter 10

The finishing touches

Your wedding day is about you as a couple, your commitment to each other and the unique bond that you share. Are you wildly romantic, fun-loving or totally traditional? Here are a few easy-to-make ideas that will create a lasting impression on your guests and will leave you with lots of lovely memories to look back on in years to come!

'Just Married' signs

These quick-make ideas will help you to decorate your venue with appropriate signs!

You might want to add these to the top table, use them to decorate the venue or even add them to the wedding transport. They're also a great way to hold on to your happy memories once the wedding day is over.

'Just Married' banner

- 🕐 Under 15 minutes per strip of two heart banners
- £ Under £2 per strip of two heart banners

Collect supplies
- ❏ Heart-shaped paper doilies
- ❏ Selection of coordinated print papers
- ❏ Pink paper streamer
- ❏ Fine-tip marker pen
- ❏ Pencil and eraser
- ❏ Paper scissors
- ❏ Template

Create the paper hearts
Draw a selection of hearts on the printed papers – the heart will sit centrally inside the paper doily. Neatly cut out each heart shape.

Construct the motifs
Using a fine-tip marker pen, sketching out in pencil first if desired, write, 'Just Married' or your chosen phrase in the centre of each paper heart. Working with a strip of paper streamer, position the doily underneath and a paper heart directly on top, and glue to sandwich the streamer.

Hang the banners
Repeat, adding the heart doilies and paper hearts to the paper streamers at regular intervals until you have the required number of strips of streamers, ready to add to your venue.

Laura's Bride Guide

Whether you have the ceremony and reception in one venue or travel on to a new location to continue the celebrations, the addition of a few newlywed signs is great for really setting the tone. Speak to the wedding coordinator at the venue or ask a member of your bridal party to take responsibility for adding these finishing touches.

Wooden 'I Do' hanging hearts

- 🕐 Under 15 minutes per heart
- £ From £2 per heart

Collect supplies
- ❏ Two small wooden hanging hearts
- ❏ Pencil and eraser
- ❏ Fine-tip black marker pen
- ❏ Coloured marker pen

Sketch your design
Using the pencil, mark out a border of dots and dashes around the outer edge of each heart. Write the words 'I Do' on one heart, and 'Me Too' on the other.

Draw the outline
Switching to the fine-tip marker pen, work over your design neatly on each heart until all the outlines have been added.

Finish with coloured accents
Use the coloured marker pen to add in accent colours to the outline of the design. When both hearts are completed they're ready to hang in your venue.

▶ These little hanging hearts will look fantastic on your wedding day, and will be perfect decorations for your Christmas tree too!

Memento boxes

Create a storage box to secure your precious memories from your wedding day.

You'll find there are a number of different trinkets and tokens from your Big Day that you'll want to hold on to and treasure for years to come. Rather than shelling out for a wedding memento box you can make a more personal version for a fraction of the cost!

Decorated memento tin

🕐 Under 1 hour, including drying time

£ From £3 per tin

Collect supplies

❏ Large metal tin – old biscuit or sweet tin
❏ Spray paint
❏ Ribbon
❏ Silk flower
❏ Small luggage tag
❏ Pencil
❏ Marker pen
❏ Strong glue
❏ Newspaper

Paint the tin

Ensure the surface of the tin is clean and dry and cover your work surface with newspaper. Working in a large, well-ventilated area, spray the sides of the tin with short, even bursts of paint. Continue rotating and spraying the tin until the entire surface is painted. Leave to dry fully.

Colour the lid

With the lid placed upright on the covered surface, begin spraying in short, even bursts of paint until the entire surface is covered. Allow to dry fully. Check that both the tin and the lid are fully covered – apply a second coat of paint if required.

Embellish the tin

Cut a length of ribbon long enough to wrap over the lid of the tin. Secure two ends to the inside of the lid at opposite sides with a dab of strong glue and allow to dry. Position the silk flower in place on the top of the lid, with its stem under the ribbon.

Use dabs of glue to secure in place. Add your preferred memento wording to the luggage tag with the black marker pen and position it on the tin lid with the flower and secure in place with strong glue.

Laura's Bride Guide

Whilst making the invitations, buttonholes and other small details for our wedding, I made an extra one of each item. I tucked these away into an old biscuit tin. After the wedding we collected together all the lovely cards, best wishes notes and little trinkets from our special day and added them to this collection. It's a great keepsake!

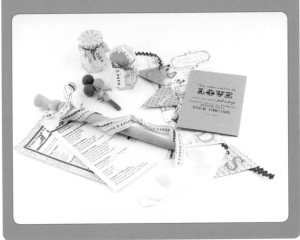

'Thank You' gifts

Present your bridal party with handmade gifts. Here are some easy-make ideas to inspire you.

Rather than handing out the customary floral bouquets here are a few different gifts you can make and give to your special guests to show your gratitude.

Homemade limoncello

🕐 Under 10 minutes – allow up to two weeks for making limoncello
£ From £3 per bottle

Make your own limoncello

My husband and I like to make limoncello every year to give as Christmas gifts – and it always goes down a treat! Here's how we make it.

- 1 litre of vodka
- 500g (17oz) caster sugar
- 6 large unwaxed lemons
- Lemon squeezer
- Large pan
- Large jar
- Sieve

Method

1 Peel the lemons, scrape away as much white pith from the underside as possible and set aside.

2 Put the caster sugar into the large pan and add 200ml of water. Over a low heat continue stirring until the sugar has dissolved.

3 Add in the lemon peel to the syrup and allow to simmer for 20 minutes.

4 Squeeze the juice from the peeled lemons and add to the syrup, allowing to simmer for another 10 minutes.

5 Remove the pan from the heat and leave to cool for 20 minutes.

6 Pour the lemon syrup mixture into the jar and add in the vodka. Leave for two weeks in a cool place, and shake the contents every two days.

7 Strain the limoncello and decant into small bottles.

Collect supplies

- ☐ Homemade limoncello decanted in bottle
- ☐ Two glasses
- ☐ 'Thank You' ribbon
- ☐ Decorative glass cubes
- ☐ Luggage tag
- ☐ Pencil and eraser
- ☐ Fine-tip black marker pen
- ☐ Coloured marker pens

Create the tag

Sketching out in pencil first, add a border of dots and dashes to the edge of the label.
Write 'Limoncello' and the date of your wedding on the centre of the tag. Work over the design using the fine-tip black marker pen.

Add ribbon

Cut a generous length of 'Thank You' ribbon – for a more professional finish aim to cut the ribbon after a complete sentiment, rather than cutting though a word. Wrap around the neck of the bottle. Feed the tag on to the ribbon before securing into a bow.

Complete the presentation

Add a couple of decorative glass cubes to the glasses and set with the bottle into a gift bag ready to be presented.

Embroidered vintage handkerchief

⏱ Under 2 hours
£ From £1 per handkerchief

Collect supplies
❑ Vintage handkerchiefs
❑ Embroidery needle and threads
❑ Small embroidery hoop
❑ Air-erasable pen

Mark out the design

Ensure the vintage handkerchief is clean and neatly pressed. Using the air-erasable pen, write out the message, keeping the lettering to an even height and spacing. Vintage linens often already have pretty stitched motifs – if yours do, place the lettering around these to emphasise them.

Secure in a hoop

Place the section of fabric to be stitched into an embroidery hoop, ensuring that the fabric is held taut and that the design is in the centre of the frame. Begin at the left-hand side of the lettering, and work using back stitch following the shape of each letter.

Complete the design

Working carefully to ensure that the back of the handkerchief is as neat as possible, complete the stitched words. Weave the thread ends into the lettering to secure and trim. Place a soft towel over the stitching before pressing to avoid damaging the stitches.

▶ Mum's of the bride and groom will find themselves welling up as you exchange your vows, so adding 'Mum' to the stitched design is a lovely thoughtful gift they'll really cherish!

Pretty potted plant

⏱ Under 10 minutes per plant
£ From £5 per plant

Collect supplies
❑ Small potted plant
❑ Coloured doily
❑ Print ribbon
❑ Small stick (cakepop or lolly stick)
❑ Strip of printed paper
❑ Alphabet stamps and ink or fine-tip black marker pen
❑ Strong glue

Wrap the pot

Place the flowerpot in the centre of the doily and bring the paper up around its sides. Hold in place with dabs of strong glue until fully secured.

Create the message

Fold the thin strip of paper in half, aligning the two short edges, and trim into a swallowtail. With the alphabet rubber stamp set or using the fine-tip blank marker add 'Thank You', or your chosen message. Position the strip around the top of the stick and glue in place to create a small flag.

Add a bow

Wrap the ribbon around the centre of the doily-wrapped flowerpot and hold in place with strong glue. Push the small 'Thank You' flag into the soil of the plant pot ready to gift.

Laura's Bride Guide

A handy bag will make gifts a little bit more manageable at the reception. Decorate plain gift bags with ribbon and a handmade tag for a custom finish that matches your wedding theme and colours.

'Thank You' cards

Let your guests know how much you appreciate their generosity with these four ideas for handmade cards.

Once the excitement of the wedding and the honeymoon has passed you'll be turning your thoughts to the generosity of your guests. Taking the time to hand-make the 'Thank You' cards and write a personal message inside them will be greatly appreciated by those who gave you gifts to mark your marriage.

Bunting card

🕐 Under 15 minutes per card
£ Under £3 per card

Collect supplies
❑ Cream-coloured card blank
❑ Selection of print papers
❑ Alphabet rubber stamp set
❑ Glue
❑ Sewing machine or needle and thread

Create the paper pennants
From the selection of coloured papers, cut out eight small triangles. Mix and match from a range of different prints or alternate between the colours and shades used for you wedding theme.

Add the lettering
Using the alphabet stamp and ink, print the letters for your 'Thank You' message on to the pennants. Aim to keep the lettering central

and towards the lower portion of the paper pennant so that it'll be clear of the stitching when it's secured.

Affix the pennants
Arrange the pennants across the card to create the effect of draped bunting. Hold in place with a small dab of glue only at the tip of each flag. Using the sewing machine or a needle and thread, stitch across the upper sections of the paper to secure the bunting.

Personalised newlywed card

🕐 Under 40 minutes per card
£ Under £1 per card

Collect supplies
❑ Natural card blank
❑ Pencil and eraser
❑ Marker pen
❑ Fine-tip black pen
❑ Coloured marker pen in two coordinating shades

Create border
Mark out border on the front of the card in pencil, using a pattern of dots, dashes and mini heart motifs. When you're happy with the design work over it using the fine-tip black pen.

Add message
In pencil write the message 'Thank You', and personalise with 'from Mr & Mrs...'. Work over in black marker pen, creating a calligraphy effect.

Use larger-tip pen for the big words and smaller-tip pen for the names.

Finish with coloured accents
Using the fine-tip coloured pens, work around the 'Thank You' message, first in the darker shade and then in the lighter shade, with a series of small dots to add a flash of colour to finish.

Photograph postcard

- Under 10 minutes per card
- £ Under £1 per card

Collect the supplies
- ❏ A photograph of the bride and groom (either a picture taken on the day or a favourite snap of you as a couple)
- ❏ Backing card trimmed to 5mm larger than photograph
- ❏ Printed ribbon
- ❏ Strong glue
- ❏ Two small brads
- ❏ Small hole punch

Add the motif
Trim the ribbon to the required lengths. You can trim the ribbon to a single sentiment, or create a border using more ribbon. Decide upon the placement on your card.

Secure the ribbon
Mark out the placement of the ribbon and create two small holes in the photograph, one at either end of the ribbon. To avoid damaging the photo use

a mini hole punch or place the card on a soft surface and pierce with a needle. Secure the ribbon in place with the brad and fasten at the back of the image.

Mount the card
Carefully position the embellished photograph on to the backing card and glue in place to secure. This card is created like a postcard for you to write your message on the back. Alternatively, you can position the image on the front of a pre-folded card and write your note on the inside.

▶ Many wedding photographers suggest taking a shot of the bride and groom together specifically to be used for 'Thank You' cards, so why not make up a small sign that says 'Thank You'? Have chat with your photographer – chances are they'll have some creative ideas that'll work for you!

▶ Don't have time to make lots of cards? There are a number of online photo services that can print images into custom 'Thank You' cards.

Rubber-stamped card

- Under 10 minutes per card
- £ Under £3 per card

Collect supplies
- ❏ Pearlescent card blank 7.6cm x 7.6cm
- ❏ Vintage print paper 6.5cm x 6.5cm
- ❏ Purple card 6.5cm x 6.5cm
- ❏ Large heart tag motif rubber stamp
- ❏ 'Thank You' motif rubber stamp
- ❏ Rubber stamp inks
- ❏ Lace-effect tape
- ❏ 3cm of white raffia ribbon
- ❏ Paper glue
- ❏ Paper scissors
- ❏ Hole punch

Stamp the motif
Using the large heart rubber stamp and ink, stamp the motif on to the purple card and, once the ink has dried, repeat to stamp the 'Thank You' motif in the centre.

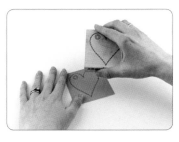

Once the ink is fully dry, carefully cut around the motif and punch a hole in the upper edge.

Create the card backing
Position the vintage paper in the centre of the card, ensuring the border around the edge is even on all sides, and glue in place. Cut a length of

lace-effect tape, peel off the backing and position across the width of the lower card, overlapping the backing paper as you work. Press into position.

Add the finished motif
Loop the raffia ribbon through the hole in the heart and secure. Affix the motif to the centre front of the card with glue. The motif will sit slightly above the backing paper. The inside of the card is left blank for you to write your message.

Templates

Use these templates to add your very own special touches to your handmade wedding. These templates can be scaled up or down and mixed and matched to create your own unique handcrafted designs.

Triangular bunting

● Cut two fabric pieces per pennant.

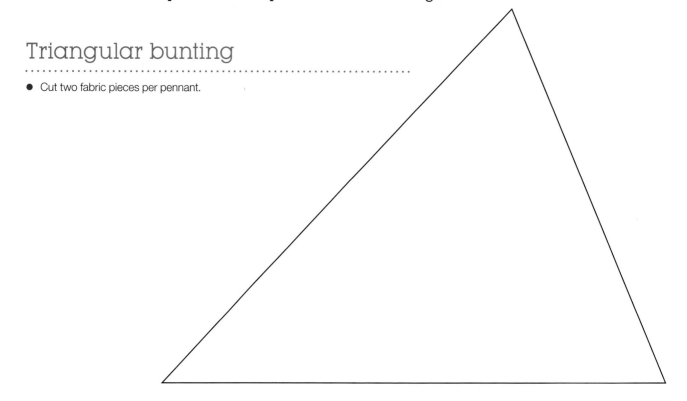

Rounded bunting

● Cut two fabric pieces per pennant.

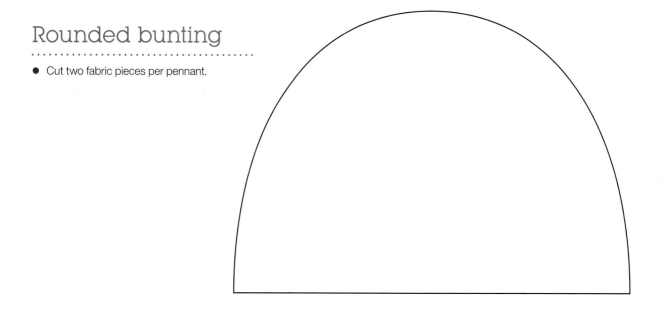

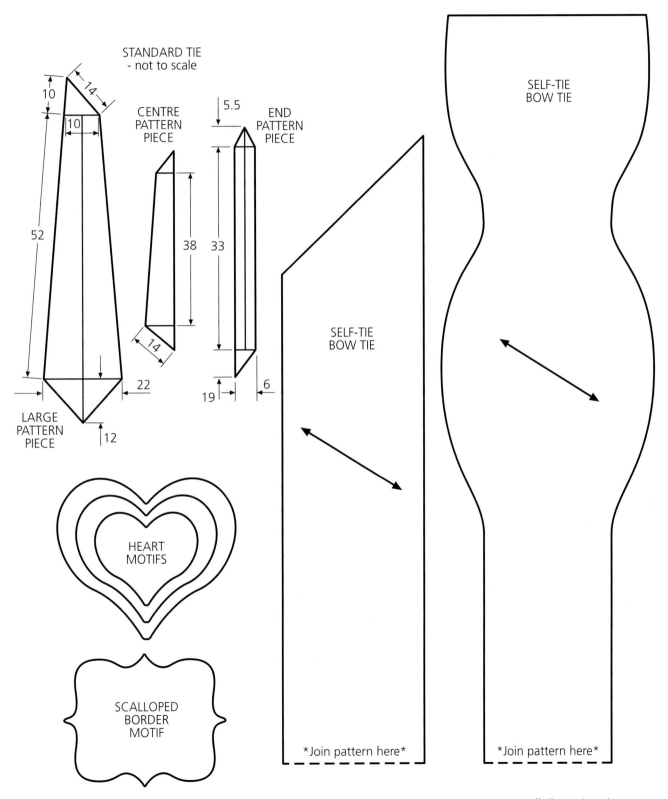

STANDARD TIE
- not to scale

10

14

10

CENTRE
PATTERN
PIECE

5.5

END
PATTERN
PIECE

SELF-TIE
BOW TIE

52

38

33

14

22

19

6

12

LARGE
PATTERN
PIECE

SELF-TIE
BOW TIE

SELF-TIE
BOW TIE

HEART
MOTIFS

Join pattern here

Join pattern here

SCALLOPED
BORDER
MOTIF

All dimensions in cm

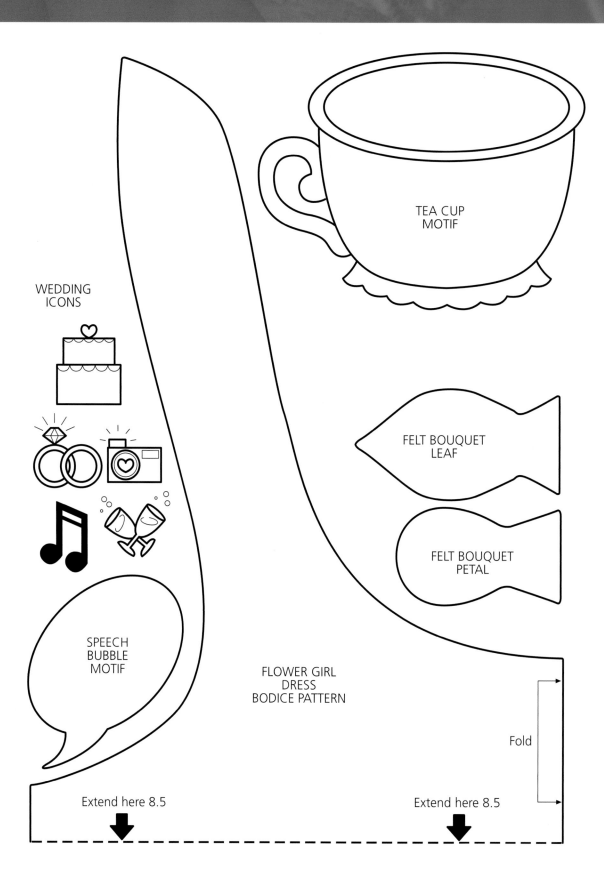

TEA CUP
MOTIF

WEDDING
ICONS

FELT BOUQUET
LEAF

FELT BOUQUET
PETAL

SPEECH
BUBBLE
MOTIF

FLOWER GIRL
DRESS
BODICE PATTERN

Fold

Extend here 8.5

Extend here 8.5

All dimensions in cm

Useful Addresses

Getting your hands on just the right supplies or vendor will take the stress out of your DIY wedding. From florists to formal wear hire, and cupcakes to craft supplies, this list will help you to find the items you need to create your own special day.

Wedding resources

- Planning a religious ceremony – www.yourchurchwedding.org
- Planning a civil ceremony – www.gov.uk/ search births deaths & marriages.
- Outdoor wedding ceremonies – www.onelifeceremonies.co.uk
- Same sex marriages – www.civilpartnershipinfo.co.uk and www.gay-friendly-wedding-venues.com
- Alcohol licensing – www.gov.uk/alcohol-licensing
- Wedding website hosting service – www.gettingmarried.co.uk
- Kerrie Mitchell Photography – www.kerriemitchell.co.uk
- James Hasler, toastmaster – www.toastmasterjameshasler.co.uk
- The Guild of International Professional Toastmasters – www.guildoftoastmasters.co.uk
- The Guild of Professional Toastmasters – www.guild-of-toastmasters.co.uk
- The Alliance of Toastmasters – www.allianceoftoastmasters.co.uk
- The Federation of Professional Toastmasters – www.federationtoastmasters.fsnet.co.uk
- The Institute of Toastmasters of Great Britain – www.institutetoastmastersgb.fsnet.co.uk
- The National Association of Toastmasters – www.natuk.com
- The Executive Guild of Toastmasters and Town Criers – www.theexecutiveguildoftoastmasters.co.uk
- The Toastmasters and Master of Ceremonies Federation – www.toastmasters-tmcf.co.uk
- The Association of English Toastmasters – www.englishtoastmasters.co.uk
- The Big Cheese Cake Company – www.hrhbigcheesecakecompany.co.uk
- The Liverpool Cheese Company – www.liverpoolcheesecompany.co.uk
- The House of Cheese – www.houseofcheese.co.uk
- The Cheese Factor – www.cheese-factor.co.uk
- The Cheese Shed – www.thecheeseshed.com
- The British Cheese Board – www.britishcheese.com
- D.Byfords & Sons Florist Wholesaler – www.byfords.co.uk
- Dream Bus Wedding Transport – www.dreambus-hereford.com
- The Red Bus Wedding Transport – www.theredbus.co.uk

Craft resources

- Made Peachy – www.madepeachy.com
- Abakhan, North Wales, Chester, Birkenhead, Liverpool, Manchester, Preston, Bolton & Hanley (Stoke-On-Trent) – www.abakhan.co.uk.
- All the Fun of the Fair – www.allthefunofthefair.bigcartel.com
- Berisfords – www.berisfords-ribbons.co.uk
- The Norfolk Candle Company – www.norfolkcandleco.co.uk norfolkcandlecompany@gmail.com
- Blooming Felt – www.bloomingfelt.co.uk.
- Dremel – www.dremel.co.uk for information on the Dremel range, and www.dremeldirect.co.uk for online orders.
- Hobbycraft – www.hobbycraft.co.uk
- Tor Coatings – www.tor-coatings.com
- Spoilt Rotten Beads – www.spoiltrottenbeads.co.uk.
- Lakeland – www.lakeland.co.uk
- Download & Print – www.downloadandprint.com
- Starblaze – www.starblaze.co.uk

First published February 2014

A catalogue record for this book is available
from the British Library

ISBN 978 0 85733 381 0

Library of Congress control no. 2013955821

Haynes Publishing,
Sparkford, Yeovil, Somerset BA22 7JJ, UK
Tel: +44 (0) 1963 442030
Fax: +44 (0) 1963 440001
E-mail: sales@haynes.co.uk
Website: www.haynes.co.uk

Haynes North America, Inc.,
861 Lawrence Drive, Newbury Park,
California 91320, USA

Printed in the USA by Odcombe Press LP,
1299 Bridgestone Parkway, La Vergne, TN 37086

Author:	Laura Strutt
Project Manager:	Louise McIntyre
Copy editor:	Ian Heath
Design and layout:	James Robertson
Wedding Photography:	Kerrie Mitchell
	www.kerriemitchell.co.uk
Project Photography:	Thomas F J Ford
	www.thomasfjford.com
Stock photos:	Shutterstock

Author acknowledgements

There are a number of people that have made the writing of
this book possible:

Kerrie Mitchell for her exceptional photography skills that
transformed our wedding day and have added delight to the
pages of this book.

To my dear family and in-laws; the Styles, Cruickshank
and Coomber families, and the Strutt, Foulkes, Newton,
Blackmore and Kennedy families, who've all listened, given
advice and guidance on weddings (our own and in this book)
for the best part of two years!

And, last but by no means least, my husband John Strutt,
for without him having made me the best offer of my life and
then becoming my husband on the 15 September 2012,
I would never have experienced the magic of creating our own
wonderful DIY wedding day.